Intermediate Excel

EXCEL ESSENTIALS BOOK 2

M.L. HUMPHREY

TITLES BY M.L. HUMPHREY

CONTENTS

INTRODUCTION

In *Excel for Beginners* we covered almost all of what you need to know to work in Excel on a daily basis. But there are additional things that I use Excel for that weren't covered there, mostly because I think sometime it just gets overwhelming when you're trying to learn something new to have everything thrown at you all at once. So the beginner's guide was meant to let you master the basics. Things like how to input data, how to format it, some basic ways to manipulate it, and how to print the results.

In this guide, which I'm calling *Intermediate Excel*, we're going to take all of that base knowledge one step further. It still doesn't cover all of Excel, but by the time we're done here I think you'll know 98% of what you'll ever want to know about Excel and probably some that you never wanted to know.

So what specifically are we going to cover?

1. Conditional Formatting
2. Inserting Symbols
3. Pivot Tables
4. Subtotaling and Grouping Data
5. Charts
6. Removing Duplicate Entries
7. Converting Text to Columns
8. The CONCATENATE function
9. The IF function
10. The COUNTIFS function
11. The SUMIFS function
12. The TEXT function
13. How to Limit the Input Choices in a Cell
14. Locking Cells or Worksheets
15. Hiding a Worksheet
16. Creating a Two Variable Analysis Grid

Also, we'll discuss how to find the answer when you want to do something I haven't covered. (I suspect that will mostly occur when you're dealing with a specific function since there are hundreds of them and I'm only covering the ones I use most often.)

This isn't a hands-on guide like *Excel for Writers*, *Excel for Self-Publishers*, or the *Juggling Your Finances Basic Excel Primer*. We're not going to put these techniques to real-world use or build the worksheets I show you as examples. But there will be lots of screenshots so you can see exactly how it all works and, me being the talkative person I am, I'll mention for each one how I've used it in the past or am currently using it.

One more thing to point out before we begin. This guide is written using Excel 2013. If you're using a version of Excel prior to Excel 2007 some of what I'm going to cover will not be available to you or it will work differently. This wasn't as much of an issue with *Excel for Beginners* as it is here, so even if you managed to get through that guide with an older version of Excel, you may not make it through this one without challenges. For example, the COUNTIFS and SUMIFS functions were introduced with Excel 2007 and Pivot Tables and Charts have definitely become easier to use in newer versions of Excel.

Alright. Let's review our basic terminology and then we'll dive into the fun stuff.

BASIC TERMINOLOGY

Column

Excel uses columns and rows to display information. Columns run across the top of the worksheet and, unless you've done something funky with your settings, are identified using letters of the alphabet.

Row

Rows run down the side of the worksheet and are numbered starting at 1 and up to a very high number.

Cell

A cell is a combination of a column and row that is identified by the letter of the column it's in and the number of the row it's in. For example, Cell A1 is the cell in the first column and first row of a worksheet.

Click

If I tell you to click on something, that means to use your mouse (or trackpad) to move the arrow on the screen over to a specific location and left-click or right-click on the option. (See the next definition for the difference between left-click and right-click).

If you left-click, this selects the item. If you right-click, this generally creates a dropdown list of options to choose from. If I don't tell you which to do, left- or right-click, then left-click.

Left-click/Right-click

If you look at your mouse or your trackpad, you generally have two flat buttons to press. One is on the left side, one is on the right. If I say left-click that means to press down on the button on the left.

If I say right-click that means press down on the button on the right. (If you're used to using Word or Excel you may already do this without even thinking about it. So, if that's the case then think of left-click as what you usually use to select text and right-click as what you use to see a menu of choices.)

Spreadsheet

I'll try to avoid using this term, but if I do use it, I'll mean your entire Excel file. It's a little confusing because it can sometimes also be used to mean a specific worksheet, which is why I'll try to avoid it as much as possible.

Worksheet

This is the term I'll use as much as possible. A worksheet is a combination of rows and columns that you can enter data in. When you open an Excel file, it opens to worksheet one.

Formula Bar

This is the long white bar at the top of the screen with the $f\chi$ symbol next to it.

Tab

I refer to the menu choices at the top of the screen (File, Home, Insert, Page Layout, Formulas, Data, Review, and View) as tabs. Note how they look like folder tabs from an old-time filing system when selected? That's why.

Data

I use data and information interchangeably. Whatever information you put into a worksheet is your data.

Select

If I tell you to "select" cells, that means to highlight them.

Arrow

If I say that you can "arrow" to something that just means to use the arrow keys to navigate from one cell to another.

A1:A25

If I'm going to reference a range of cells, I'll use the shorthand notation that Excel uses in its formulas. So, for example, A1:A25 will mean Cells A1 through A25. If you ever don't understand exactly what I'm referring to, you can type it into a cell in Excel using the = sign and see what cells Excel highlights. So, =A1:A25 should highlight cells A1 through A25 and =A1:B25 should highlight the cells in columns A and B and rows 1 through 25.

With Formulas Visible

Normally Excel doesn't show you the formula in a cell unless you click on that cell and then you only see the formula in the formula bar. But to help you see what I'm referring to, some of the screenshots in this guide will be provided with formulas visible. All this means is that I clicked on Show Formulas on the Formulas tab so that you could see what cells have formulas in them and what those formulas are.

Unless you do the same, your worksheet will not look like that. That's okay. Because you don't need to have your formulas visible unless you're troubleshooting something that isn't working.

Dialogue Box

I will sometimes reference a dialogue box. These are the boxes that occasionally pop up with additional options for you to choose from for that particular task. Usually I include a screen shot so you know what it should look like.

Paste Special – Values

I will sometimes suggest that you paste special-values. What this means is to paste your data using the Values option under Paste Options (the one with 123 on the clipboard). This will paste the values from the cells you copied without also bringing over any of the formulas that created those values.

Dropdown

I will occasionally refer to a dropdown or dropdown menu. This is generally a list of potential choices that you can select from. The existence of the list is indicated by an arrow next to the first available selection. I will occasionally refer to the list of options you see when you click on a dropdown arrow as the dropdown menu.

CONDITIONAL FORMATTING

Alright then. Let's dive right in with a conversation about conditional formatting.

What is it and why would you want to use it?

At its most basic, conditional formatting is a set of rules you can apply to your data that help you see when certain criteria have been met. I, for example, use it in my budget worksheet where I list my bank account values. I have minimum balance requirements on my checking and savings accounts, so both of the cells where I list those values are set up with conditional formatting that will color those cells red if the balance in either account drops below the minimum requirement. This helps remind me of those requirements, because I'm not always thinking about it when I move money around.

Conditional formatting is also useful when you have a set of data and want to easily flag certain results as good or bad. You can combine conditional formatting with filtering so that you first apply your conditional formatting to your data to color the ones you want to focus on and then filter the data using Cell Color or Font Color.

The easiest way to see how conditional formatting works is to walk through an example.

	A	B	C	D	E	F	G	H	I	J	K
1	Sale Price	$ 4.99									
2	Payout	70%									
3							Monthly Sales Per Title				
4					15	30	60	150	250		
5				1	$ 52.40	$ 104.79	$ 209.58	$ 523.95	$ 873.25		
6				2	$ 104.79	$ 209.58	$ 419.16	$ 1,047.90	$ 1,746.50		
7				3	$ 157.19	$ 314.37	$ 628.74	$ 1,571.85	$ 2,619.75		
8				4	$ 209.58	$ 419.16	$ 838.32	$ 2,095.80	$ 3,493.00		
9				5	$ 261.98	$ 523.95	$ 1,047.90	$ 2,619.75	$ 4,366.25		
10				6	$ 314.37	$ 628.74	$ 1,257.48	$ 3,143.70	$ 5,239.50		
11				7	$ 366.77	$ 733.53	$ 1,467.06	$ 3,667.65	$ 6,112.75		
12				8	$ 419.16	$ 838.32	$ 1,676.64	$ 4,191.60	$ 6,986.00		
13				9	$ 471.56	$ 943.11	$ 1,886.22	$ 4,715.55	$ 7,859.25		
14				10	$ 523.95	$ 1,047.90	$ 2,095.80	$ 5,239.50	$ 8,732.50		
15											
16											
17											

Conditional Formatting (Red<$1500, Green>$3500)

(Number of Titles — vertical label on left of data rows)

This one is pulled from *Excel for Self-Publishers* and is a two-variable analysis grid that looks at the various combinations of number of titles and monthly units sold per title to project a monthly income number. (It actually uses four variables because it's set up so you can also change the assumed list price and payout in the top left corner, but the grid itself is comparing the combinations of titles and number sold. We'll talk about how to build a generic two-variable grid like this one later.)

I've applied conditional formatting to the results to flag in red any cell where the monthly income would be less than $1,500 and to flag in green any cell where the monthly income would be over $3,500.

To color the cells green if the amount is over $3,500, I highlighted the cells I wanted to apply conditional formatting to (in this case E5:I14), then went to the Styles section of the Home tab and clicked on the dropdown arrow next to Conditional Formatting. I then choose Highlight Cells Rules and Greater Than.

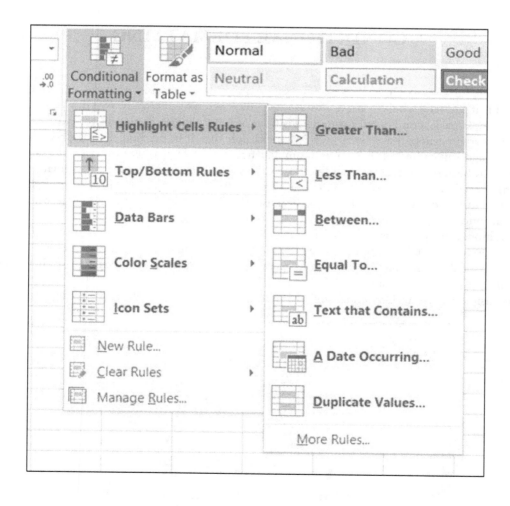

This brought up the Greater Than dialogue box where I entered 3500 in the left-hand field and chose Green Fill with Dark Green Text from the right-hand dropdown.

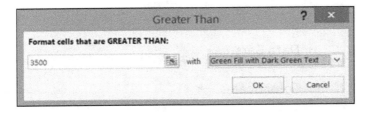

After I clicked OK any cell where the value was greater than $3,500 was colored green with green text.

To color the cells red if the amount was under $1,500 I did the same thing except I chose Less Than under Highlight Cells Rules and entered 1500 in the left-hand field of the Less Than dialogue box.

To sum it up: Highlight your cells, go to the Styles section of the Home tab, click on Conditional Formatting, choose the option you want, set your parameter, and choose your desired formatting.

With the Highlight Cells Rules, you can set parameters using Greater Than, Less Than, Between, Equal To, Text that Contains, A Date Occurring, or to flag Duplicate Values.

I should note that the duplicate values option doesn't discriminate between different values. So if you have a 7, 8, and 9 repeated twice in a list it will color all of the 7s, 8s, and 9s in the list the same color. (We'll talk later about how to remove duplicate values from a list if you need to.)

The date option is a bit odd as well. It lets you flag a date occurring yesterday, today, tomorrow, in the last seven days, last week, this week, next week, last month, this month, or next month. Depending on what you want to use it for, those options could be very useful or very limited.

With the highlight cells rules I usually stick with the default formatting options of Light Red Fill with Dark Red Text, Yellow Fill with Dark Yellow Text, Green Fill with Dark Green Text, Light Red Fill, Red Text, or Red Border. But note that there is also an option at the bottom of that dropdown menu to apply a custom format. When you click on that option it brings up the Format Text dialogue box. With that you can basically format the cell however you want. I was just able to choose to format my text with a purple font and in italics.

There are other options available to you other than the Highlight Cells Rules. The next one on the list is Top/Bottom Rules. You can format values that fall in the top X of your range, the bottom X of your range, the top X% of your range, the bottom X% of your range, above the average for the range, or below the average for the range. (While the options are labeled Top 10 Items, Top 10%, etc. when you click on them you'll see that you can adjust the number to whatever you want to use.)

The next option you have is to add Data Bars to your cells. With data bars, the higher the value, the longer the bar within the cell. It creates a quick visual representation of relative value.

Color Scales are another way to show the relative value of cells within a range. With Color Scales the color moves from red for smaller values through yellow and to green for the larger values.

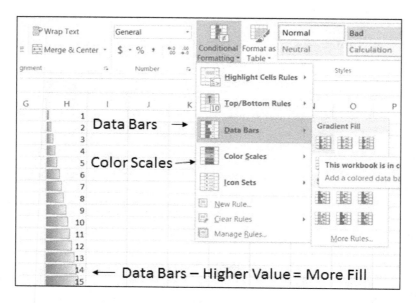

In the Data Bars example above, I had the values in order so you could easily see the bars getting bigger as the numbers increased in size. Here's an example of Data Bars and Color Scales with the data in order versus in a random configuration:

Your last option is Icon Sets which insert a colored symbol into each cell based on its relative value within the range. (See image below for an Icon Set that uses a non-filled, half-filled, or fully-filled star to demonstrate relative value.)

If you want to use Data Bars, Color Scales, or Icon Sets but you want to set absolute limits for when a color is applied (as opposed to letting Excel look at the data and divide it equally), you can do so by highlighting the cells you've applied the conditional formatting to and going to Manage Rules under Conditional Formatting in the Styles section of the Home tab and then choosing Edit Rule. This will let you set the parameters for each criteria.

In the examples below you can see that I've edited the default criteria:

You can always remove any conditional formatting from a range of cells or a worksheet by going to the Conditional Formatting dropdown, choosing Clear Rules, and then choosing to clear all rules from a range of cells or from the entire worksheet.

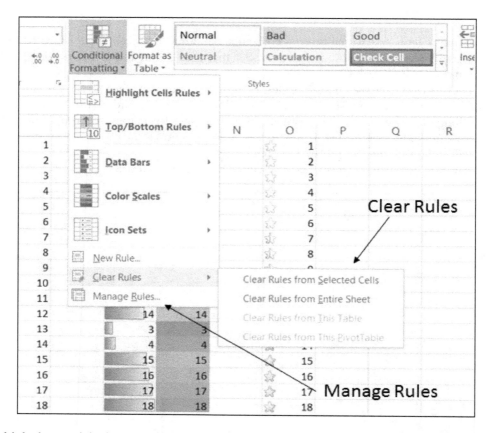

If you think there might be conditional formatting you want to keep and you just want to remove one rule, go to Manage Rules instead, which will show you all of the conditional formatting rules that are in place on the worksheet. (You can choose to display all rules for the worksheet using the dropdown at the top of the dialogue box.)

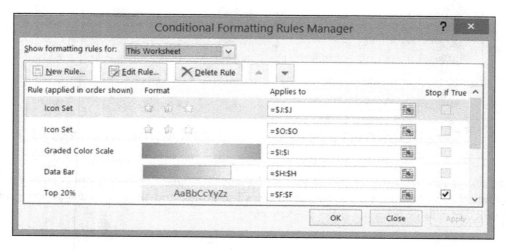

You can also change the order of the rules, edit them, or create new ones from here.

Be careful if you have multiple rules running that could conflict with one another that they're set to run in the correct order and that you've considered whether or not to check the "Stop if True" box. (If that box is checked, then the minute that criteria is met in that cell, none of your other rules will run on that cell.)

And, last but not least, you can also go to New Rule from the Conditional Formatting dropdown to add any type of rule you want to add, including all of the ones we just discussed. This will bring up the New Formatting Rule dialogue box. It's probably the best place to go to create complex rules with custom parameters, but it won't be as user-friendly as the dropdowns. (Like with all things in Excel, the options you can access from the dropdowns on the tabs are what you'll need most often, the dialogue boxes are where you go to do everything else.)

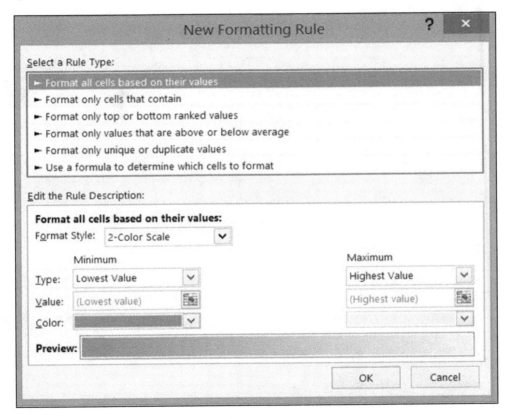

Finding which option you want will be the biggest challenge, but after that it's just a matter of making your choices from the dropdowns and specifying your limits and thresholds in the provided fields.

Now on to something much simpler: Inserting Symbols.

INSERTING SYMBOLS

This doesn't come up often, which is why I included it in this book instead of the beginner book. But I do occasionally want to insert a symbol into a field. For example, maybe I want to use the € sign for Euros or the £ sign for British Pounds. There are shortcuts you can type that will insert them, but I don't do it often enough to know them.

Another time I've used symbols is in my tracking of my short story submissions which I covered in *Excel for Writers*. In that case I used stars and exes to indicate which stories had received personal rejections from a market and which had received form rejections.

Inserting a symbol is a very straight-forward process. You can either insert a symbol into its own cell or as part of text within a cell. Like this:

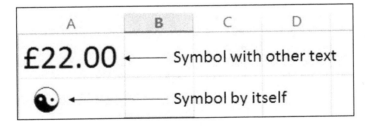

In Cell A1 I inserted a symbol and then clicked into the cell and typed my additional text. (I could've just as easily done so in the opposite order.) In Cell A2 I simply inserted my chosen symbol.

Once a symbol is there, you can treat it just like text and change the font size or the font color. DO NOT change the font, though. For a lot of these that's what determines the symbol you're seeing. For example, that yin yang symbol is actually what a [looks like in the Wingdings font.

So how do you do this?

Simple. First, click into the cell where you want to add the symbol. (If there's already text in that cell, then click into the spot within that text in the formula bar where you want to add the symbol.) Next, go to the Insert tab and click on Symbol in the Symbols section. This will bring up the Symbol dialogue box:

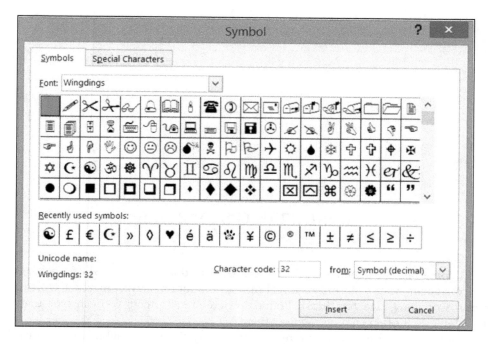

If you've recently used the symbol you're looking for it will be under Recently Used Symbols at the bottom of the dialogue box. Otherwise, you can scroll through the displayed symbols which will give you most language-based symbols like Greek and Coptic, Cyrillic, Armenian, Hebrew, and Arabic as well as currency symbols and arrows and a lot of other basic choices.

If that doesn't have what you're looking for, change the Font in the dropdown menu. Wingdings fonts are the ones that tend to have images like scissors, mailboxes, smiley faces, Zodiac symbols, etc.

Note that there's also a Special Characters tab where you can find things like the copyright symbol, trademark symbol, and paragraph symbol.

When you find what you're looking for, click on the symbol so that it's highlighted and then click on Insert at the bottom of the dialogue box. In the cell where you inserted the symbol you will see the symbol as an image, but in the formula bar it will appear as the normal text symbol it is in a font like Times New Roman. So for example, below I inserted an asterisk but in the font Ennobled Pet. In the Cell it appears as a paw print with an asterisk in the center. In the formula bar you just see the asterisk.

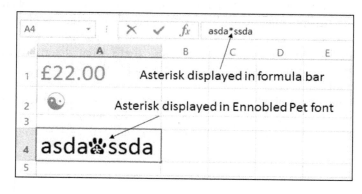

That's it. It's that simple. Just remember that a lot of the symbols you'll insert are driven by the font choice, so if you do insert symbols into your file be very careful about using the Format Painter or selecting all and changing the font, because you may end up erasing any symbol you inserted.

PIVOT TABLES

Alright. Now that we had a breather, let's dive back into one of the most useful things you can do in Excel, which is create a pivot table of your data. A pivot table takes rows and rows of data and puts it into nice summary reports based on the criteria you set. I use these all the time. If you only learn one thing from this guide, let it be pivot tables.

If you're self-published, they're great for summarizing the Amazon daily and monthly sales reports. In less than a minute you can see what sales you have by title or how much you've earned in each currency or how many page reads you've had. I also use it to see my ad spend by title, month, or author.

If you're not self-published, pivot tables can be used on any listing of data where you have more than one entry per customer or product or whatever. So, say you run a small business and had 1,000 sales this year and now you want to know who your best customer was and all you have is those 1,000 entries. You could sort by customer and then manually add up sales for each one, which could take hours. Or you could create a pivot table that calculates total sales for each customer and then sort to see who's at the top and be done in less than five minutes.

Sounds great, right? So how do they work? What do you do?

First, you need your information organized in the right format. There needs to be one row that contains the labels for each column. (I sometimes call this the header row.) Directly below that you need to list your information with one row per entry and nothing else other than the data.

The mistake a lot of people make (and Amazon used to do with their monthly reports which they have now fortunately changed) is that they'll list information in one row and then below that row list a subset of information. So maybe Row 5 is the customer information and then below that they list the transactions for that customer in Rows 6-10 and then Row 11 is another row of customer information and below that are the transactions for that customer.

The problem with that approach is that you can't easily manipulate that data. You can't sort it, filtering it is a challenge, you can't use pivot tables with it, and you can't create charts from it either. It's information that's there for display purposes not analysis.

Don't do that.

At least not in your source worksheet.

Always have one place where you simply list your information. You can then use that worksheet to create your summary reports and analysis. But always have that one document that is just the information.

Also be sure not to have any blank rows or columns in your data set and to have only one type of data (date, currency, text) per column. (Blank rows aren't a deal-breaker, but Excel will treat them as valid sources of data so you'll end up with blank entries in your summary tables. Blank columns will generate an error message when you try to create the pivot table.)

To understand the proper way to display your data, let's look at an example:

	A	B	C	D
1	Albert Jones			
2		8/1/2015	1 widget, 1 other	$25.00
3		8/30/2015	10 widgets	$250.00
4		9/1/2015	3 whatchamacallits	$45.00
5				
6	Richard Martinez			
7		3/7/2016	10 who knows what	$35.00
8		4/7/2016	20 whatsits	$30.00
9				
10				
11				

Bad Data Layout

G	H	I	J	K	L
Customer	Date of Transaction	Quantity	Item	Unit Price	Total
Albert Jones	8/1/2015	1	Widget	$ 20.00	$ 20.00
Albert Jones	8/1/2015	1	Other	$ 5.00	$ 5.00
Albert Jones	8/30/2015	10	Widget	$ 25.00	$ 250.00
Albert Jones	9/1/2015	3	Whatchamacallit	$ 15.00	$ 45.00
Richard Martinez	3/7/2016	10	Who knows what	$ 3.50	$ 35.00
Richard Martinez	4/7/2016	20	Whasit	$ 1.50	$ 30.00

Good Data Layout

On the top is a display of information that you can't do anything with. Look at customer Albert Jones. How many units has he bought total? How many widgets vs. whatchamacallits? And overall, how many widgets have you sold this year? And to whom? You'd have to physically calculate those numbers because of the way they were recorded. (This is fine for a final report, but it shouldn't be how you store that information initially.)

In contrast, look at the bottom example. It's the same information. But now if we want to know how many widgets Mr. Jones has bought we can just filter that list by customer and widget. (Or we can create a pivot table which we'll do in a moment.) Same with overall number of units sold for the year. Just add a quick formula and you have your answer.

So what are the rules? How should you structure your data to get the most use out of it?

To the extent you can, when you're listing information, have a separate column for anything you might want to analyze or use to separate your data. So here, for example, we have customer name, date, and item in separate columns, because we may want to use those to separate our data. We also have quantity of each item, unit price, and total paid in separate columns because we might want to use each of those values to calculate numbers such as how much customers spend or how much they pay per unit on average.

Also, try to standardize entries to the extent you can. (Later we'll talk about using data validation to limit the allowed values within a cell.) A widget should always be called a widget. Don't let it be called a blue widget sometimes and a red widget other times or enter it as widget once and widgets the next time. (If colors matter, create a column for color or use a product code to distinguish the two.)

And don't have extra summary lines or columns mixed in with your raw data. So don't have a row inserted in the midst of your sales entries that totals up the values for Customer A. (All of that should happen in another worksheet. This should just be where you store your raw data.)

Use one row, ideally Row 1, to label each of your columns and identify what that column contains, and then one row for each transaction with all the details you want to track in that one row. This may mean you repeat information, such as customer name in multiple rows. That's fine. (Just be sure it's standardized and Customer A is always written the same way.)

The analysis you can perform depends one hundred percent on how you structure your data.

Okay, then. Assuming you have a good set of data to work with, it's time to create a pivot table.

Highlight your data. (If it's the entire worksheet, you can Select All by clicking in the top left corner. If the data starts lower down in the worksheet, be sure to highlight the header row as well as the data rows.)

Go to the Insert tab and choose Pivot Table.

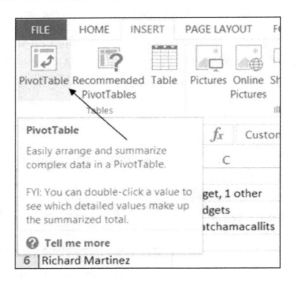

Choose to add your Pivot Table to a new worksheet. (I always do this because I don't want my source data and my pivot table to interfere with one another.) After you do so, you should see a blank pivot table on the left-hand side and a listing of the available pivot table fields on the right-hand side.

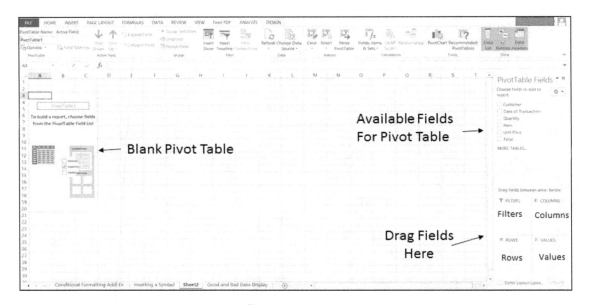

Click on the name of each of the fields you want to use and either drag each field to the table on the left or to the area in the bottom right corner where it says "Drag fields between areas below." I prefer to drag them downward, but both ways work.

In this example I dragged Customer to the Rows section and Quantity and Total to the Values section. This gave me a pivot table where I could see quantity bought and total paid by customer.

	A	B	C
1			
2			
3	Row Labels	Sum of Quantity	Sum of Total
4	Albert Jones	15	320
5	Richard Martinez	30	65
6	Grand Total	45	385
7			

For any field you drag to the Values section, be sure that the correct function is being performed on the data. I have some data sets (Amazon's) that I work with where the default is to Count numbers instead of Sum them. If you need to change the function being performed on the data, click on the arrow next to the field name and choose Value Field Settings.

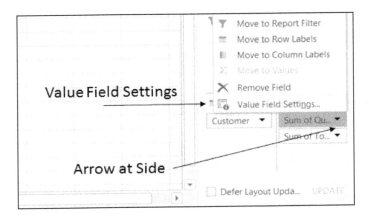

This will bring up the Value Field Settings dialogue box where you can choose to display the results as a Sum, Count, Average, Minimum, Maximum, Product, Count Numbers, or Standard Deviation. You can also choose on the Show Values As tab to show the result as a % of the Grand Total, % of the Column Total, % of the Row Total, and many other options.

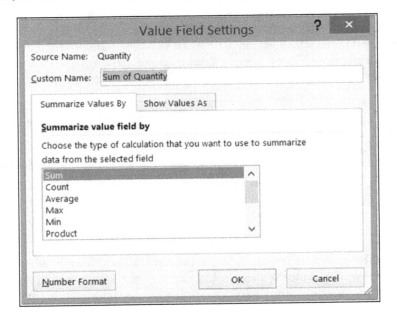

In the Value Field Settings dialogue box you can also choose how to format the values in that column of the table by clicking on the Number Format box at the bottom. (You can also format the cells by highlighting them and using the Number section of the Home tab to choose your format or by highlighting them, right-clicking, and choosing Format Cells.) In this example, I've set up the Quantity column to display as % of Column and formatted the Total column as Currency.

If you want to perform two (or more) calculations with the same field, just add it more than once and specify for each instance the function you want performed.

You can also add variables to go across the top of the table as well. Below I've added Item into the Columns section of the pivot table. Since I had two entries listed in the Values section, it creates two columns for each Item.

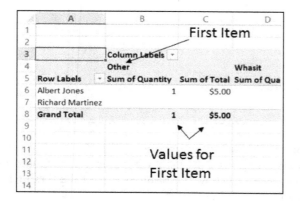

If you don't like the order that your entries are in, you can right-click on an entry and use the Move option to change the display order. You can do this within the values for each variable (so I could move Other to the end in the above example) or when you have multiple column or row variables.

If I remove Unit Price from Values, then it's a much simpler table to view. Here we have Item across the top, customer down the side, and the units of each item bought by each customer in the table:

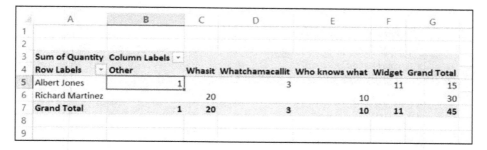

You can also filter the results in your pivot table so that it's specific to a subset of your data. To apply a filter, you move the field you want to filter by into the Filters section and then choose the values you want from the drop down menu. Uncheck any values you don't want included in the table.

For example, here I moved Item to the Filters section and then unchecked all items except Whatchamacallits. (The easy way to do this is click the box next to (All) so that all values are unselected and then choose the one you want.)

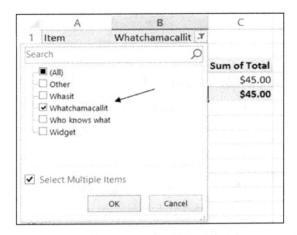
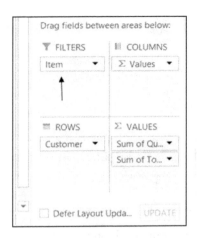

There are a number of other things you can do with pivot tables using the Analyze tab under PivotTable Tools. (If you aren't seeing PivotTable Tools, click on the pivot table in the worksheet.)

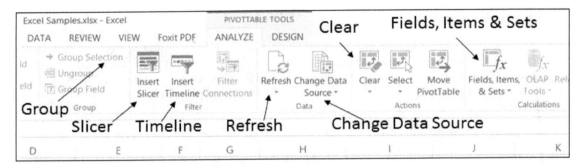

* * *

You can create an artificial grouping of entries by clicking on each of the items you want to include in the group while holding down the Ctrl key and then choosing Group Selection from the Group section of the Analyze tab. To remove a grouping, click on the Group name and then choose Ungroup.

Once you've grouped a set of results (say books in a series or related customer accounts), you can click on the minus sign next to the group name and that will hide the individual entries that make up that group and only display the totals for the group.

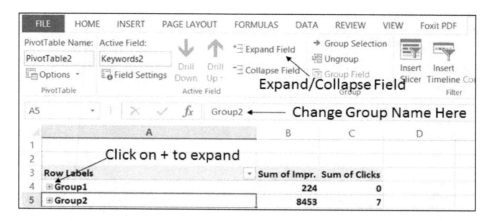

To rename a group, click on its name and then change the group name in the formula bar.

Clicking on Collapse Field in the Active Field section of the Analyze tab will collapse all grouped entries into their summary row. Clicking on Expand Field will expand all of them.

* * *

I've never used Insert Slicer before, but it seems to basically work like a filter option, without being a filter. So you can choose to insert a slicer, click on the field you want to slice by, and then click on the values for that field that appear in the slicer box and it will narrow your pivot table down to just the results that match that criteria. To undo your slice, click on the funnel image in the top right corner of that box.

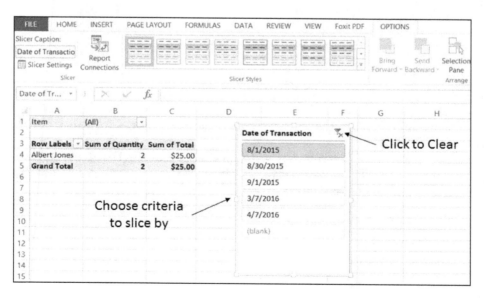

* * *

Insert Timeline is another one I've never used before. It appears to use any date provided in your data and let you narrow it down by month, quarter, year, or day. This is very handy for data where you have just the date (8/9/15) but want to see the data by month or year without having to add new fields to your original data source. (And certainly beats my old method of filtering by date and then checking/unchecking boxes.)

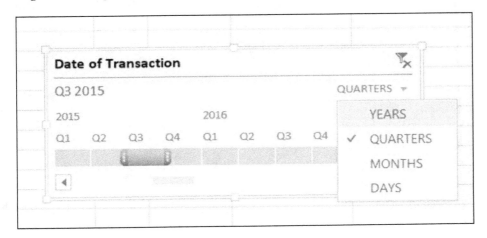

* * *

You can use Refresh to update the table if your source data changes. For example, you might find that customer Albert Jones was entered as Albert Jones and Albert R. Jones so is showing as two different entries. After you go back to your source data and update one of the entries, click on Refresh to have Excel regenerate the table to reflect the change.

* * *

You can also use Change Data Source to change the data the pivot table includes. For example, if you've added additional entries since it was last generated. Click on Change Data Source and then Change Data Source in the dropdown menu and it will take you to the page with your source data as well as highlight the cells contained in that range. The easiest way to update the range is to use your cursor to select all of the cells you want in range. If you have thousands of rows of data, you can select the top section of the data and then click into the box and change the final number to correspond to the last row of your data. (If you try just updating the cell references by typing in the data field, it sometimes gets messed up and tries adding cell ranges within your existing range, so I usually avoid that approach.)

* * *

If you want to keep the pivot table but start over fresh by removing all fields and settings, you can click on Clear, and choose Clear All. To clear just the filters you've applied to the table, click on Clear and choose Clear Filters.

* * *

If you want to add a new calculation to the table (for example, I usually want to place a dollar value on my page reads which requires multiplying them by a constant), you can do so using Fields, Items, & Sets. Click on it and choose Calculated Field. You'll see a dialogue box where you can name the field and build a calculation using existing fields and/or other numbers. Here I've calculated a tax due amount using a 5.75% tax:

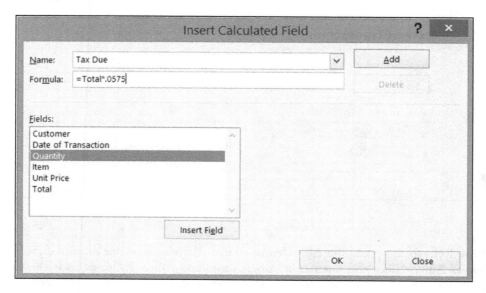

When you're done, click on OK. The field should be listed in your Pivot Table Fields and may already be shown in your table. If it isn't showing in your table, drag it to where you want it to be and change any value field settings you need to change. (So that, for example, it sums the values instead of counts them.)

* * *

The Design tab under Pivot Table Tools allows you to choose how the table displays. You can change the color, add a blank row after every entry in the table, choose when and how to display subtotals, choose when and how to display grand totals, and change the formatting of the row and column headers. It basically allows you a number of options to refine your table results to display according to your preferences. For example:

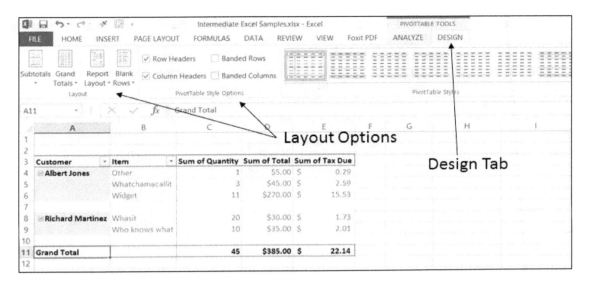

Here I've chosen to change the color, add a line between entries, display the column grand totals, not display subtotals or row totals, and I've kept the bolded row and column headers.

What else?

To remove a field you didn't want to add to the table, click on the arrow next to the field name in the bottom right corner and choose Remove Field. You can also right-click in a cell in a column in the table and choose Remove [Column] to remove a column from the table. Or right-click on a row value and choose Remove [Row] to remove a row from the table. (I use brackets there because the option will actually name the row or column you're allowed to delete. So, it'll say "Remove Units" for the Units variable.)

If you have multiple entries under Row, Column, or Values and want to change their order, left-click and drag the field to where you want it.

To undo something you just did and didn't like, click anywhere in the worksheet and use Ctrl + Z. (It won't work until you've clicked into the worksheet for whatever strange reason.)

One thing to be cautious of when working with pivot tables is that they're dynamic. The number of rows is not set and the number of columns can easily change based upon your choices of what to include or not include in the table. This is the reason I tend to build them as I need them but not keep them long-term. If you do set one up that you want to repeatedly run, which I can see doing if you get fancy with your settings, just be careful that (a) you always have all the data you want to include selected and (b) that you don't add other text or calculations around the table that could be overwritten or become inaccurate when the table is refreshed. (You'll see if you try to write a formula referencing an entry in a pivot table that it isn't just referencing that cell, it's referencing the pivot table and an entire subset of the data in the table based upon the listed criteria. So you might write a formula in Row 6 that corresponds to Customer Jones who is currently listed in Row 6 but then refresh your table and Customer Jones is now in Row 8 but the formula is still in Row 6 and still refers to Customer Jones.)

My advice if you want to do additional calculations on your data is to either copy the entire table and paste special-values and then do your analysis on that pasted table, or to build the calculations into the table itself as discussed above. Don't mix the two. Don't create a pivot table and then do external computations on those values while it's still a pivot table.

Alright.

Hopefully that was a good, solid beginning with respect to pivot tables. If you want to go further with them, your best bet is the Microsoft website at https://support.office.com.

(The big topic I didn't cover here is how to link multiple tables of data to create one pivot table. That's very close to what you do in Access, and it would probably require an entire book of its own. I muddle my way through in Access, but it's not something I'd feel comfortable teaching, so we're going to put that one under the heading Advanced Excel Topics, a book I will never write.)

SUBTOTALING AND GROUPING DATA

While pivot tables are a great way to analyze a table of data, they're not the only way. In a moment we'll talk about charts, which are a visual way of analyzing data. But first let's talk about something much more simple: the ability to subtotal data.

I like to use this for my monthly income numbers. I have a table that lists month, year, units sold, and amount earned. With subtotals I can easily take that listing and see what I earned and sold for each calendar year.

You could just as easily use subtotals to get summary information by customer or product.

The Subtotal option is located in the Outline section of the Data tab.

To subtotal your data, first sort it by the criteria you want to use to group your data. Here's our sample data:

	A	B	C	D
1	Month	Year	Units	Amount Earned
2	August	2013	1,234	$ 346.51
3	September	2013	2,345	$ 426.21
4	October	2013	3,456	$ 524.23
5	November	2013	23,454	$ 1,199.90
6	December	2013	24,565	$ 32,932.77
7	January	2014	25,676	$ 40,507.30
8	February	2014	26,787	$ 1,475.88
9	March	2014	4,567	$ 1,815.33
10	April	2014	5,678	$ 2,232.86
11	May	2014	6,789	$ 644.81
12	June	2014	7,900	$ 793.12
13	July	2014	13,455	$ 975.53

I want to subtotal my data by year, so I've sorted it to make sure that all of the 2013 entries are together, all the 2014 entries are together, and all the 2015 entries are together. (I actually sorted by year and then by month because I'm compulsively anal like that, but sorting by year was all that was needed.)

If you don't sort your data before you try to subtotal it, you'll end up with something like this when you do subtotal:

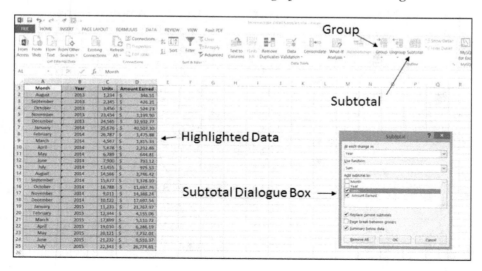

There are two entries for 2014 and 2015 because the data wasn't sorted by year, so I had a couple of rows of 2015 data interspersed with my 2014 data. Each time the year changed, Excel treated it as a new group.

So remember, with subtotals *you always need to sort your data first.*

Alright. Now that your data is sorted, select all the fields with data in them and click on Subtotal in the Outline section of the Data tab. This should bring up the Subtotal dialogue box.

First, under "at each change in" choose which column you want to group on using the dropdown menu to select that column's name. (You can have subtotals of multiple columns, but you can only group the data by one column.)

Next, choose what function you want to use for subtotaling the other columns. (Usually the function I want is Sum, but you can also choose Count, Average, Max, Min, Product, etc.)

Finally, under "add subtotal to" check which columns you want that function to be performed on. In this case, we want it to be for units and earnings.

Once you've done that, you can then choose whether you want each grouping to appear on its own page by checking the box for "page break between groups", whether you want the summary of the entire column at the very bottom by checking "summary below data", and (if you had existing subtotals), whether you want to replace any existing subtotals by checking "replace current subtotals."

Once you're satisfied with your choices, click OK.

You should end up with something like this:

	Month	Year	Units	Amount Earned	
1	**Month**	**Year**	**Units**	**Amount Earned**	
2	August	2013	1,234	$ 346.51	
3	September	2013	2,345	$ 426.21	
4	October	2013	3,456	$ 524.23	
5	November	2013	23,454	$ 1,199.90	
6	December	2013	24,565	$ 32,932.77	
7		**2013 Total**	55,054	$ 35,429.62	
8	January	2014	25,676	$ 40,507.30	
9	February	2014	26,787	$ 1,475.88	
10	March	2014	4,567	$ 1,815.33	
11	April	2014	5,678	$ 2,232.86	
12	May	2014	6,789	$ 644.81	
13	June	2014	7,900	$ 793.12	
14	July	2014	13,455	$ 975.53	
15	August	2014	14,566	$ 2,746.42	
16	September	2014	15,677	$ 3,378.10	
17	October	2014	16,788	$ 11,697.76	
18	November	2014	9,011	$ 14,388.24	
19	December	2014	10,122	$ 17,697.54	
20		**2014 Total**	157,016	$ 98,352.89	
21	January	2015	11,233	$ 21,767.97	
22	February	2015	12,344	$ 4,155.06	
23	March	2015	17,899	$ 5,110.72	
24	April	2015	19,010	$ 6,286.19	
25	May	2015	20,121	$ 7,732.01	
26	June	2015	21,232	$ 9,510.37	
27	July	2015	22,343	$ 26,774.61	
28		**2015 Total**	124,182	$ 81,336.93	
29		**Grand Total**	336,252	$ 215,119.45	
30					

See those numbered columns on the left-hand side? Those are your group levels. In the image above, we're looking at all of the rows of data.

If I click on the 2 in the top-left corner, I will only see one row per year without any of the detail rows showing. Like this:

		Month	Year	Units	Amount Earned
	1				
+	7		2013 Total	55,054	$ 35,429.62
+	20		2014 Total	157,016	$ 98,352.89
+	28		2015 Total	124,182	$ 81,336.93
−	29		Grand Total	336,252	$ 215,119.45
	30				

And if I were to click on the 1 I would only see the Grand Total row. What we've done here is taken a table of data and grouped it by year and subtotaled the units sold and earnings for each of those years.

To remove subtotals, go back to the Subtotal option and click on Remove All in the Subtotal dialogue box.

If you want to keep the subtotals, but remove the groupings on the left-hand side, you can either click on Ungroup in the Outline section of the Data tab and then select Ungroup once more. (This will remove one level of grouping at a time.) Or you can click on Ungroup and then choose Clear Outline, which will remove all levels of grouping.

* * *

Alright, that was Subtotals. Now on to Groups.

The Group option allows you to group rows or columns so that you can easily hide them or show them once again by simply clicking on a plus or minus sign.

This is similar to hiding columns or rows in terms of what it does, but it's much more useful for situations where you have columns or rows that you'll be routinely hiding and unhiding.

So how to do it:

The columns or rows you group have to be adjacent. (So this doesn't work the same as with pivot tables.)

Select all of the rows or columns you want grouped, choose Group from the Outline section of the Data tab, and then choose Group again from the dropdown.

When you've successfully grouped columns or rows you'll see a section above or to the side of the worksheet with numbers for each group level and a minus sign. (If you close the group, that minus sign will become a plus sign.)

Here I've grouped my first two columns and you can see the minus sign above them when they're visible and the plus sign above Column C when they're not. You can hide or unhide those columns by clicking on the plus or minus sign. It's that easy.

Month	Year	Units	Amount Earned					Units	Amount Earned
Click to Hide Group								**Click to Show Group**	
August	2013	1,234	$ 346.51					1,234	$ 346.51
September	2013	2,345	$ 426.21					2,345	$ 426.21
October	2013	3,456	$ 524.23					3,456	$ 524.23
November	2013	23,454	$ 1,199.90					23,454	$ 1,199.90

To remove all grouping from a worksheet use Clear Outline under Ungroup in the Outline section of the Data tab.

One final note: Ctrl + Z and Ctrl + Y did not always work for me when I was subtotaling and grouping data while writing this section. I had two Excel files open at the time and when I tried to undo something related to subtotaling or grouping it sometimes undid something in the other worksheet instead of the subtotaling or grouping I'd just done. So my advice is use the Remove All and Clear Outline options instead when dealing with subtotaling and grouping.

CHARTS – DISCUSSION OF TYPES

Charts are a great way to visualize your data. There's nothing like a nice bar chart or pie chart to see exactly what's going on. You know what they say, a picture's worth a thousand words. And seeing one big chunk of color dominating all the others tells you everything you need to know about who your best customer is or what your biggest expense is.

Just like with pivot tables, your data needs to be arranged properly before you can use charts. Specifically, for most of the charts we're going to discuss, you need one set of labels across the top and one set down the side with values listed in the cells where those two intersect.

Here are two examples:

Data Table Option 1

	Amazon	Createspace	ACX	Con Sales
201701	$100.00	$37.00	$23.50	$10.00
201702	$107.00	$39.59	$25.15	
201703	$114.49	$42.36	$26.91	
201704	$122.50	$45.33	$28.79	$25.00
201705	$131.08	$48.50	$30.80	
201706	$140.26	$51.89	$32.96	$8.00

Data Table Option 2

	201701	201702	201703	201704	201705	201706
Amazon	$100.00	$107.00	$114.49	$122.50	$131.08	$140.26
Createspace	$37.00	$39.59	$42.36	$45.33	$48.50	$51.89
ACX	$23.50	$25.15	$26.91	$28.79	$30.80	$32.96
Con Sales	$10.00			$25.00		$8.00

This is fictitious sales data for each month for various sales platforms. In the first example, the sales channels are listed across the top and the months are listed along the side with the intersection of those two showing the dollar value of sales for that sales channel for that period.

In the second example, each month is listed across the top and each of the sales channels is listed down the side.

(My version of Excel will work with your data in either configuration, but I'm pretty sure that's not how it used to be.)

To create a chart from your data, highlight the cells that contain your labels and values. In the examples above that would either be G1:K7 or M1:S5.

Go to the Insert tab and click on the Chart type you want. (See next section for a detailed discussion of chart types.) As soon as you place your mouse over each chart selection you'll see the chart appear. When you click on that selection, the chart will be inserted into your worksheet.

We'll discuss each chart type in detail next, but the general rule is that for time series data like the examples above that include multiple variables (your sales channels) across multiple time periods (each month), the best choices are column charts, bar charts, and line charts. For data where you have multiple variables but no time component, a better choice is a pie or doughnut chart. Scatter charts are good for random data points where you're looking at the intersection of two or three variables to see if there's any sort of relationship between them.

Excel does offer additional chart types like bubble charts and radar charts, but we're not going to cover them in this guide.

Okay, time to discuss Column Charts, Bar Charts, Line Charts, Pie and Doughnut Charts, and Scatter Charts in more detail.

Column Charts

The top-left chart option in the Charts section of the Insert tab is Column Charts. It's the image with the upright bars.

There are seven possible column charts that you can choose from, but I'm going to focus on the top set of choices, which are the 2-D versions since most of the 3-D versions are the same except three-dimensional.

For 2-D, you can choose from clustered columns, stacked columns, and 100% stacked columns. Here is an example of all three using the exact same data:

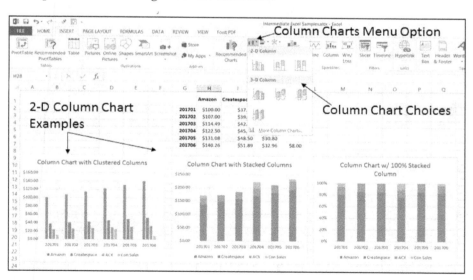

The difference between the clustered columns and the stacked columns is that the clustered columns version puts the results for each variable side-by-side for each time period. You can easily see the height difference between different results, but it can quickly become too busy if you're dealing with a large number of variables. For example, I have nine sales channels I track. Having nine columns side-by-side for each of twelve months would be overwhelming.

In that case, the stacked columns option is a better choice. Like with clustered columns, stacked columns have different column heights for each variable based on their value, but the columns are stacked one atop the other instead of side-by-side for each time period. So you end up with only one column per time period.

The stacked columns option lets you see the overall change from time period to time period based on the total height of the column.

The 100% stacked columns option presents all of the information in one column just like stacked columns does. But instead of basing each section's height on its value, it shows the variable's percentage share of the whole. While you lose any measurement of value (a column chart with values of 2:5:5 will look the exact same as one with values of 20:50:50 or 200:500:500), you can better see changes in percentage share for each variable. (A variable that goes from 10% share to 50% share will be clearly visible.)

As mentioned above, the first three 3-D column chart options are the same as the 2-D options. The only difference is that the bars are three-dimensional instead of two-dimensional. (And really that's more of a gimmick for Powerpoint presentations than anything else. Remember: Charts should be as clean and simple as you can make them while still presenting all necessary information.)

The final 3-D option is a more advanced chart type that creates a three-variable graph, and we're not going to cover that in this guide. (Consider it an Advanced Excel Topic.)

Bar Charts

Bar charts are the next chart type you see under the Charts section of the Insert tab. They're just like the column charts, except on their side, with a clustered, stacked, and 100% stacked option available in both two-dimensional and three-dimensional versions.

Here are examples of the 2-D versions:

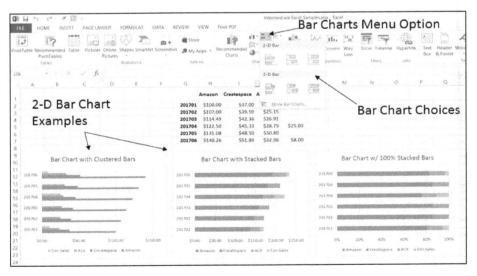

Line Charts

Line charts are the first chart type shown in the second row of choices. There are seven options listed, but you should only use the first choice on the left for each of the 2-D rows of choices.

This is because the other four 2-D options really aren't viable for a line graph. They're meant to do what the stacked columns graphs do and show relative values, but people just don't read line graphs that way. You expect that if there's a line drawn on a graph that it's showing actual values for that particular variable not relative values or cumulative values

The 3-D option is a more advanced chart type that creates an actual three-variable line graph and we're not going to cover it in this guide. (Consider it an Advanced Excel Topic.) You can use it to create a two-variable line graph with a three-dimensional line, but don't. Keep it simple.

Here are examples of the basic line chart and the line chart with markers:

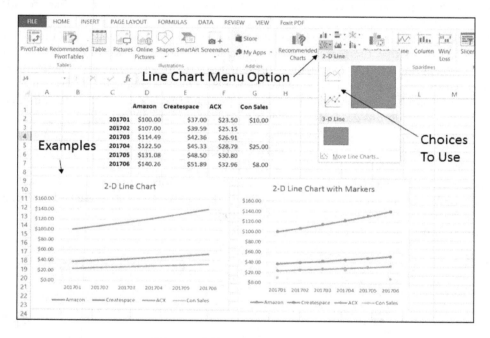

Pie and Doughnut Charts

Next we have pie and doughnut charts. These are best used when you have one set of variables for one period of time. So I've built the below examples using just the total values for each of the sales channels.

(To select a subset of your data, like I've done here, you can use Ctrl and your mouse to highlight just the sections you want before you choose your chart type. Or you can select all of the data, choose your chart type, and then go to Select Data and remove the data you don't want to use.)

There are three two-dimensional pie chart options and one doughnut chart option. The three-dimensional pie chart option is the same as the basic pie chart except in three-dimensions.

Here are examples of the two-dimensional pie charts and the doughnut chart:

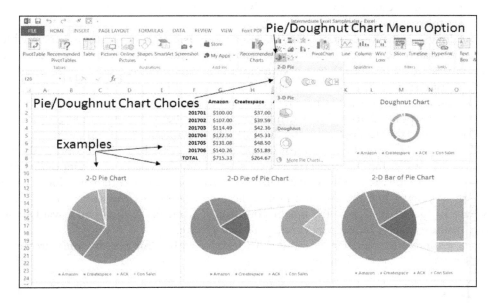

For the pie charts, you can choose between a standard pie chart, a pie of pie chart, or a bar of pie chart

If you're only focused on who or what accounts for the biggest share, then you should just use the standard pie chart or the doughnut chart.

If you want to be able to clearly see the results for all of your segments, even the smallest ones, then the pie of pie chart or the bar of pie chart are potentially better choices.

The pie of pie chart creates one main pie chart in which it combines a number of the smaller results to form one segment of the chart. It then breaks out those smaller results into their own pie chart where they each take up their proportion of that smaller part of the pie.

So, for example, in the sample we're seeing here, ACX and Con Sales were combined in the left-hand pie chart but were the only ones in the right-hand pie chart. In the left-hand chart, together they are 18% of the total. In the right-hand chart they are 78% and 22% *of that 18%*. (If you were to insert labels on this chart, the labels would be the share that each one had of the overall whole, so the smaller pie chart would show 14% and 4% as the labels. It's a bit confusing.)

The bar of pie chart does something similar except it creates a bar chart with the smaller values instead of a smaller pie chart. In order to avoid confusion, the bar of pie chart is probably the better choice of the two, but honestly I wouldn't use either one if you could avoid it. (The best charts can be read without explanation and I'm not sure that would be true for either of these for your average user.)

Scatter Charts

Scatter charts (or scatter plots) are the second option on the bottom row of the chart types.

Scatter charts plot the value of variable A given a value for variable B. For example, if I were trying to figure out if gravity is a constant, I might plot how long it takes for a ball to reach the ground when I drop it from varying heights. So I'd plot time vs. distance. From that I could eventually see that the results form a pattern which does indicate a constant. (Thanks high school physics teacher for making physics fun.)

There are five scatter plot options. The first one is a classic scatter plot. It takes variable A and plots it against variable B, creating a standalone data point for each observation. It doesn't care what order your entries are in, because there's no attempt to connect those entries to form a pattern.

The other four scatter plot options include lines drawn through each plotted point. The two smooth line options try to draw the best curved line between points. The straight line options just connect point 1 to point 2 to point 3 using straight lines between each point. The charts with markers show each of the data points on the line, the charts without markers do not.

Excel draws the line from the first set of coordinates you provide to the second to the third, etc. This introduces a time component into your data since the order you list the data points in impacts the appearance of the line. If you have data where the order of the measurements doesn't matter and you still want to draw a line through the points (like my example of dropping a ball from varying heights where it doesn't matter which height you drop it from first), then you'll want to sort your data by one of the variables before you create your scatter plot.

Here is an example of a scatter plot and a scatter plot with a line for five measurements of the time it takes for a ball dropped from different heights to reach the ground:

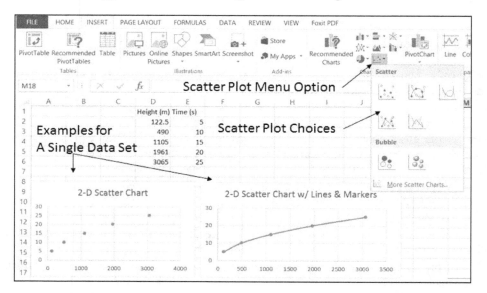

Because I sorted the data before I plotted it, we can see a nice trend line that indicates some sort of exponential relationship exists there.

You can also use scatter plots to chart more than one set of results. You just need to list the results side-by-side with the criteria you want as the horizontal axis listed first. Like this:

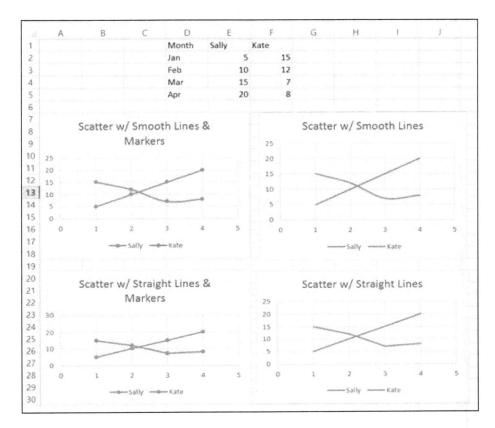

In this case we're charting the results for some measurement for two different people over the course of four months. See how the smooth line plots have lines that curve whereas the straight line plots don't? The more drastic the changes between points, the more noticeable that would become.

Note that you can also map multiple sets of data in a basic scatter plot without the lines, but including the lines makes it easier to see any difference between the data sets.

* * *

Now that you understand the basic chart types, let's talk about how to edit your charts to get them to look exactly like what you want.

CHARTS – EDITING

Chances are, once you've created a chart you'll want to edit it. With the sample charts I showed you in the last chapter I edited the name of each one, resized them, and moved them. But you can do much more than that. Like label each axis, change the legend, label your data, change the chart colors, etc. So let's walk through some of that.

* * *

We'll start with a few fixes for if the chart doesn't seem to be working the way you expected it would. These involve using Switch Row/Column, Select Data, and Change Chart Type in the Design tab under Chart Tools.

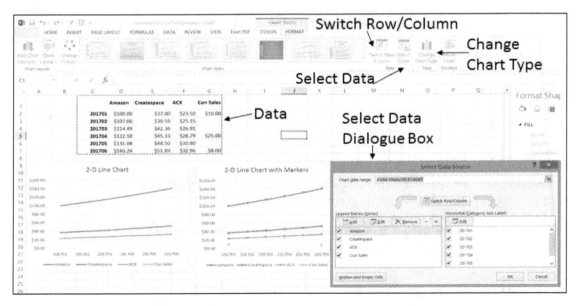

Switch Row/Column

Once you've created your chart you may find that the data you wanted along the bottom is along the side and the data you wanted along the side is along the bottom. The easiest way to fix this is to click on Switch Row/Column in the Data section of the Design tab under Chart Tools. (If you can't see the Chart Tools tabs, click onto the chart somewhere and they should appear.)

Select Data

You may also find that the data being charted isn't the data you wanted to chart. To change your data selection go to Select Data in the Design tab under Chart Tools. This will bring up the Select Data Source dialogue box. (See above.)

To remove a series of data, uncheck its box or highlight it and then click on Remove.

To add a series, click on Add, name the series, and then select the data to include from your worksheet.

To edit a series, select the series you want to edit, click on Edit, and then change the selected cells to what you want.

To change the order of the series elements, click on one of the elements and use the up and down arrows.

To remove an unwanted axis label, uncheck the box next to it.

You can also expand or reduce the data covered by a chart by clicking in the chart, going to the data table which should now be highlighted, and then left-clicking in the bottom right corner, and dragging the border of the highlighted area to either expand or contract the selection. (If you do this, just be sure that the highlight also expands for the data labels, too. It should, but if it doesn't you'll need to do so manually.)

Change the Chart Type

If you decide that you want a bar chart instead of a column chart or a column chart instead of a line chart you can click on the chart and then go to the Insert tab and choose the new chart type.

Or you can go to the Design tab under Chart Tools, click on Change Chart Type, and choose from there.

* * *

Once you have the chart you want and the data points in the places they should be, the next step is to make sure that the chart elements you want are present. For example, that data labels are included on a pie chart or a legend is included on your bar chart.

There are two easy ways to do this using Chart Styles or Quick Layouts. You can also easily change the color palette using Change Colors. All three are located in the Design tab under Chart Tools. (Be sure to click on your chart to see the Chart Tools.)

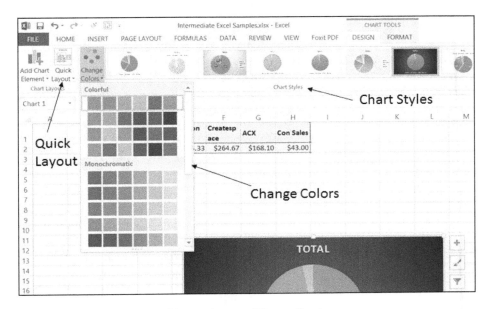

Choosing a Chart Style

Excel provides a number of pre-defined Chart Styles to choose from. The number of choices varies depending on the type of chart, but there are usually a variety with different colors and chart elements included or excluded.

To select one, click on your chart and go to the Design tab under Chart Tools. You'll see the available options in the Chart Styles section of the tab. If there are more than seven available, you can see the rest of them by using the arrows on the right-hand side of the box.

To see what a style will look like, hold your cursor over the style image. To pick a style, click on it.

(You can choose a Chart Style and then customize it further using Chart Elements and the formatting options we'll discuss in a minute, so if you see a style that's close to what you want, pick it.)

Using a Quick Layout

The Quick Layout dropdown is also in the Design tab under Chart Tools but in the Chart Layouts section. It provides a variety of layout options to choose from. The exact number will again depend on the chart type you've chosen.

The layouts include various configurations of data labels, axis labels, legends, and grid lines. (One option for scatter charts even includes an r-squared calculation.) To use a quick layout, click on your chart and then click on the one you want. If you hover over each one you can see what it will look like before you make your choice.

If you use a Quick Layout after you choose a Chart Style the color scheme and background colors will stay the same as the Chart Style, but the layout will update. If you choose a Quick Layout and then a Chart Style, the Chart Style will override your Quick Layout, so if you want to combine the two start with your chart style.

Using Change Colors

The easiest way to change the colors in your chart is to use one of the pre-defined color palettes available under Change Colors. Just click on Change Colors in the Design tab and then select the palette you want.

* * *

Add Chart Element

If you want more control over which chart elements are included and where they're positioned, but still want to work with pre-defined options, use the Add Chart Element dropdown menu in the Design tab.

The options available will vary by chart type. For example, as you can see below, Data Table, Lines, and Up/Down Bars are not available for scatter plots.

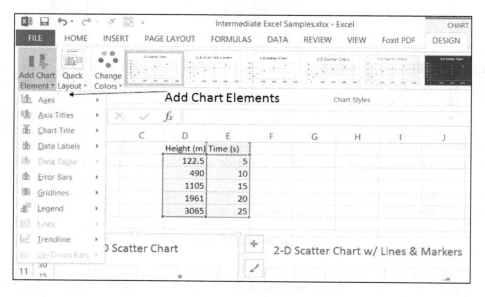

To see the possible choices for each chart element, highlight the name and a secondary dropdown menu will appear. For each of the options shown in the secondary dropdown menu, you can hover your mouse over the option to see what it will look like before you click on it and make the change.

Let's walk through what each element represents:

1. **Axes**

   Axes allows you to add (or remove) data point labels to each axis.

2. **Axis Titles**

   Axis Titles allows you to add (or remove) a title to each axis.

3. **Chart Title**

Chart Title allows you to either (a) remove the chart title entirely, (b) place it at the top of the chart, or (c) place it in a centered overlay position.

4. **Data Labels**

You can use Data Labels to label each of the data points in your chart. (I find this particularly useful with pie charts, although I usually have to move the labels from their default locations, something we'll discuss how to do in the next section.)

5. **Data Table**

Data Table allows you to add or remove a table below your chart that shows the data that was used to create the chart.

6. **Error Bars**

You can add bars that show the standard error, standard deviation, or percentage error in your data. (Usually you would use these if you had a data set that was predicting values and you wanted to show your potential error range. I wouldn't recommend using these on a chart unless you're dealing with data of that type and know what you're doing.)

7. **Gridlines**

Gridlines allows you to add (or remove) horizontal or vertical lines to your chart. These can make it easier to identify the approximate value of a specific point in the chart.

8. **Legend**

Legend allows you to determine the position of the legend (the listing of what each color in the chart stands for) within the chart. If you choose top and bottom, the legend elements will be in a row. If you choose right or left, they'll be displayed in a column. You can also remove the legend, although I generally wouldn't recommend that.

9. **Lines**

Lines allows you to add high-low lines or drop lines to a line chart.

10. **Trendline**

You can use Trendline to add a line onto your data to see if it fits a pattern like a linear or exponential relationship. (I'll note, though, that when I tried it on the data I purposefully constructed to follow an exponential pattern that it imposed a curve in the wrong direction. Honestly, I wouldn't use this unless you have a very good reason to do so.)

11. **Up/Down Bars**

You can add Up/Down bars to a line graph. Another one I wouldn't use unless you have a very specific reason for doing so.

* * *

Now that you have all of the elements in place, time to discuss how to change the aesthetics of the chart. Things like size, position, and colors.

Changing the Chart Size

If you click onto a chart you've created you'll see white squares appear at each of the corners as well as in the middle of each side. Hover your mouse over each of these squares and you'll see that the cursor turns into a two sided arrow. Left-click and drag and you can increase or decrease the size of your chart. All of the elements within the chart will resize themselves automatically to fit the new size.

Moving a Chart

If you want to move a chart within your worksheet, left-click on an empty space within the chart, hold and drag. (Don't click on an element within the chart, like the title, because that will just move that element around. If you do that, like I sometimes do, just Ctrl +Z to put the element back where it was and try again.)

If you want to move a chart to another worksheet or even another file (including a Word file or PowerPoint presentation), you can click onto an empty space within the chart and use Ctrl + C to copy it or Ctrl + X to cut it, and then Ctrl + V to paste it into the new location.

Moving Elements Within a Chart

You can manually move any of the elements within a chart by left-clicking on the element and dragging it to its new location.

Renaming a Chart

To change the name of a chart, left-click on the Chart Title. You should see the title is now surrounded by a box with blue circles in each corner. You can now highlight the existing text, delete it, and then add your own text.

Renaming a Data Field as Displayed in the Legend

To change the data labels used in the legend, you need to do so in the data table. As soon as you do that, the chart legend will update as well.

Changing the Color of Chart Elements

The easiest way to change the color of the chart elements is to use Change Colors, which we discussed above. If those colors aren't sufficient, you can use the Format tab under Chart Tools to change the color of each separate element in the chart one-by-one.

To do so, double-click on the element with the color you want to change, go to the Format tab under Chart Tools, and click on either the Shape Fill dropdown or the Shape Outline dropdown. You'll use Shape Fill for bar, column, and pie graphs and Shape Outline for 2-D line graphs. (Be careful with the 3-D line graphs, because if you use Shape Outline you'll only be changing the color on the edges of the line, not the entire line.)

Once you've clicked on the dropdown for Shape Fill or Shape Outline you can use one of those provided colors or go to More Fill Colors and choose a custom color from there.

Be sure that you've only selected the elements you want to change or you may end up changing the color of all of the elements in the chart. (Something that kept happening to me when dealing with the pie charts. If that happens, just Ctrl + Z to undo and try again.)

When you click on an element, it should by default select all of the elements in the chart that relate to that variable. If it doesn't, try again rather than manually changing each one.

Another way to change the color of a chart element is to use Shape Styles in the Format tab under Chart Tools. Be sure, as above, to only select the elements you want to change. Click on the element first and then click on the style that you want.

Using the Formatting Task Pane

The box on the right-hand side of the screen that appears when you're working in a chart gives yet another way to change your formatting. (If it isn't there, double-click on the chart or an element in the chart and that should bring it up.)

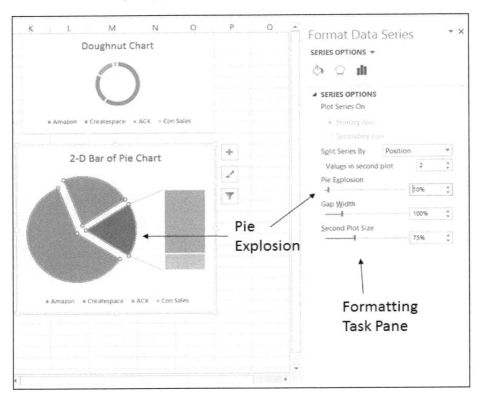

The options you'll be given vary depending on the type of chart and where you've clicked within that chart. You can do things like edit the fill style for chart elements, change the chart border, specify the size of the chart, choose how the text within the chart displays, etc.

For example, with a basic pie chart this is where you'd go to expand the pie pieces outward from the center so that the pieces have separation (pie explosion) or to rotate the pie so that the pie slice you want displayed at the top is (angle of first slice).

Changing Font Properties

If you want to change the font, font color, font size, or font style (italic, bold, underline), you can also click on the text element and then go to the Home tab and change the font options there just like you would with ordinary text in a cell.

* * *

There you have it. How to create a chart and customize for your needs. Let's move on to something a little easier now, Removing Duplicates.

REMOVING DUPLICATE ENTRIES

Sometimes I find myself with a data set that has values listed more than once, but all I really care about is the unique values. For example, you might have a listing of client transactions and want to extract from that a list of your client names. But you don't need John Smith listed three times and going through and manually deleting those duplicate entries is painful. (I'm pretty sure I used to have to do that using subtotals to help me find them...)

Anyway. It's very easy to remove duplicate entries in Excel using the Remove Duplicates option.

To do this, highlight the column of data you're working with, go to the Data tab, and click on Remove Duplicates and you'll then see the Remove Duplicates dialogue box which lets you choose which columns to remove duplicates from and to indicate whether or not your data has headers.

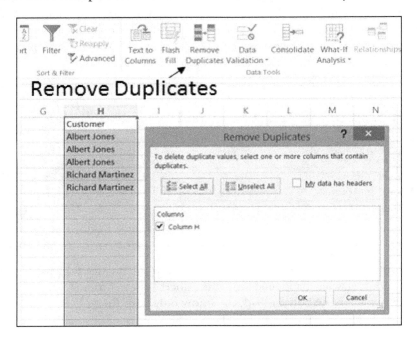

If you indicate that your data has headers, the first row of data will be excluded from the analysis. Once you've made your selections, click OK.

You'll see above that I was removing duplicates from Column H. In the results below, you can see that the multiple entries for Albert Jones and Richard Martinez were removed and that Excel condensed the entries so that they form a new list with one entry per customer and no blank lines in between.

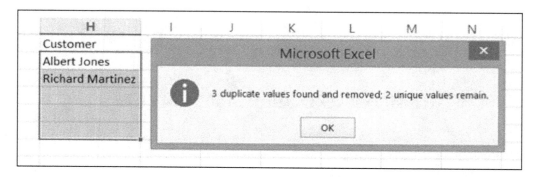

You can also use multiple columns to determine if duplicates exist. For example, you could use Customer Name and Customer State to identify duplicates in a situation where you want to keep both ABC Corp in Nevada and ABC Corp in New York as separate entries.

Whether you're using one column or more than one column, best practice is to isolate the columns you want to use into a new worksheet. The reason for this is that if you have six columns of data and only use two of those columns to remove duplicates, data in the other columns will also be deleted at the same time that Excel removes the duplicates. Which means that you only end up with one row of data per unique value set even if that's not what you wanted. And Excel won't condense that data into the remaining row. You lose that information entirely.

Here's an example of what happens. In the data set below I have five columns of data and I'm going to use two of them, Customer and Item, to remove duplicates.

	A	B	C	D	E	F
1	Customer	Date of Transaction	Quantity	Item	Unit Price	Total
2	Albert Jones	8/1/2015	1	Widget	$ 20.00	$ 20.00
3	Albert Jones	8/1/2015	1	Other	$ 5.00	$ 5.00
4	Albert Jones	8/30/2015	10	Widget	$ 25.00	$ 250.00
5	Albert Jones	9/1/2015	3	Whatcham	$ 15.00	$ 45.00
6	Richard Martinez	3/7/2016	10	Who know	$ 3.50	$ 35.00
7	Richard Martinez	4/7/2016	20	Whasit	$ 1.50	$ 30.00
8						
9						

I should end up with three entries for Albert Jones and keep the two for Richard Martinez.

And I do. But look at what happened with the Albert Jones entries. I originally had an 8/1/15 and an 8/30/15 entry where he bought Widgets. I now only have the 8/1/15 entry.

	A	B	C	D	E	F
1	Customer	Date of Transaction	Quantity	Item	Unit Price	Total
2	Albert Jones	8/1/2015	1	Widget	$ 20.00	$ 20.00
3	Albert Jones	8/1/2015	1	Other	$ 5.00	$ 5.00
4	Albert Jones	9/1/2015	3	Whatchan	$ 15.00	$ 45.00
5	Richard Martinez	3/7/2016	10	Who know	$ 3.50	$ 35.00
6	Richard Martinez	4/7/2016	20	Whasit	$ 1.50	$ 30.00
7						
8						
9						

Microsoft Excel ✕

(i) 1 duplicate values found and removed; 6 unique values remain.

OK

The other entry was removed entirely and there's no obvious way to see that that happened in the remaining data.

So, again, best practice here is to only have the columns you're going to use to remove duplicates. If you leave in other columns you will have bad data. You will either lose entire rows of information, like in the example above, or, if you choose to not expand the selection, your data will no longer match up because the columns you selected will be shorted when the duplicates are removed but none of the surrounding columns will.

Remove Duplicates is a fantastic tool. *If used properly.*

This is a good point in time to repeat one of the key rules to data analysis: Keep your source data untouched. Always work with a copy. You never know when something you do will introduce an error and you won't realize it right away. You need that clean source file to go back to when that happens.

Okay. On to Converting Text to Columns.

CONVERTING TEXT TO COLUMNS

Converting text to columns allows you to take information that's all in one cell and split it out across multiple columns. The most basic use of this is when you have something like comma-delimited data where all of the data is listed as one long entry with commas separating each piece of information, often found in a .csv file. If you want to put each piece of information into its own column, you can often just paste that data into Column A, run text to columns on it, and you'll have what looks like a normal table of data in less than a minute.

Comma-delimited data is special because it's literally built to have commas as the separator. (Sometimes it does get messy if the data entries also have commas in them, so you need to look at your data when you're converting it to see if this will be an issue for you. We'll talk about delimiters more in a second.)

I use text to columns in a very different way.

I like to use it to rearrange data or strip out information I don't need.

For example, I was recently given a listing of employees where the entire employee name for each employee was in one cell with first name followed by last name. So "Bob Smith," "Alfred Jones," "Katie Clark," etc. Because there was some variation in people's first names (Jim instead of James or a guy whose legal first name was Albert but who went by Dave), I wanted to change that list to one I could sort by last name. Text to columns allowed me to easily do that by taking those name entries and splitting each one into one column for first name and one column for last name.

Let's walk through how I did that:

First, make sure that there isn't any data in the columns to the right of the data you want to convert. Excel will overwrite any existing data you have in those other columns. If you do have data in the columns to the right of the column you're converting, you can insert columns to make space for the conversion. I'd recommend inserting a few more columns than you think you'll need. (All it takes is one Alfred David Jones, Jr. in your list to create havoc.)

Next, highlight the cells with the data you want to convert, go to the Data tab, and in the Data Tools section click on Text to Columns. This will bring up the Convert Text to Columns Wizard dialogue box which walks you through the conversion process.

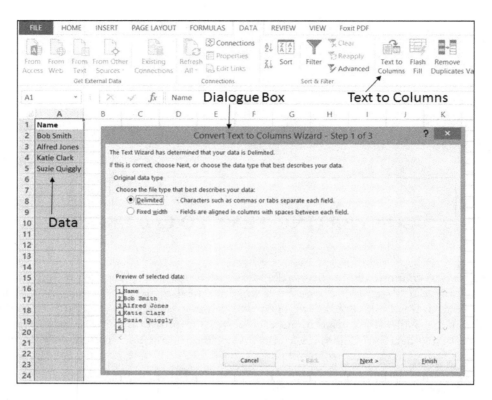

You have two options on the first screen: Delimited or Fixed Width.

Fixed Width lets you split your data into columns based upon number of characters/spaces without any consideration for what the actual content is.

Fixed Width conversion is useful when you have standardized entries that are all built the same way and you need to separate out a portion of those entries. For example, if your company uses a customer ID where the first three letters are a location identifier, you could use the fixed width option to separate the location identifier from the rest of the customer ID.

Delimited allows you to specify a character or characters that separate your data elements. (That's what I used for this example since my first and last names are of varying lengths but are separated with a space.)

Once you've selected between Fixed Width and Delimited, click on Next. This will take you to the second screen where you can set the break locations for Fixed Width or specify the delimiter(s) for Delimited.

Below is the second screen for the Fixed Width option. You can see that in the data preview section in the bottom half of the dialogue box Excel shows a sample of what the data will look like. Breaks can be of any size. Click on the data preview to place a break line, double-click to remove it, click and drag to change its position.

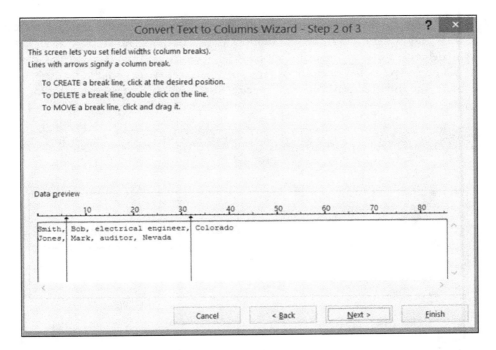

Below is the second screen for the Delimited option:

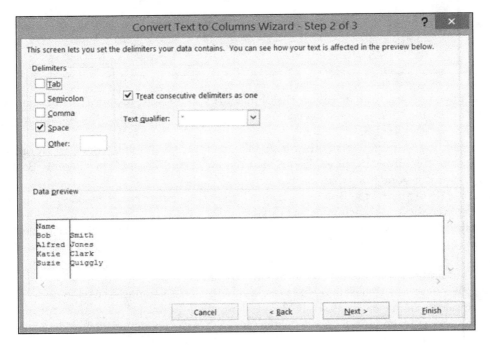

You can choose one or more of the listed options as your delimiter or specify your own delimiter using the Other option. The data preview section at the bottom shows how your data will be separated. Any delimiters that you specify will be deleted from the final data. In this example, that means there will be no spaces left in either of the two columns that are going to be created.

On the third and final screen you can specify how each of your new columns should be formatted.

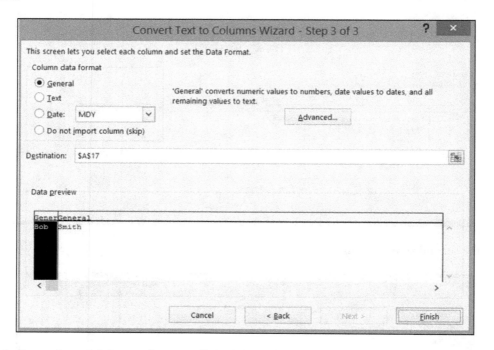

If they don't need special formatting just click Finish. If you do want to specify formatting (General, Text, Date, or do not import), you can click on that column and then select the formatting you want. Once that's done, click Finish.

You should now see that your entries have been split across multiple columns. In our example, "Bob Smith" in column A becomes "Bob" in Column A and "Smith" in Column B. The space between the words is gone since that was our delimiter.

Converting "Bob Smith" to "Bob" and "Smith" is very straight-forward and easy to do.

Not every scenario you'll encounter will be so simple.

If the names in that list had been written as "Smith, Bob" instead, then I would've had to choose both commas and spaces as my delimiters. Otherwise, if I'd just chosen commas as the delimiter it would have keep that space between the two words and I would've ended up with "Smith" in Column A and both a space and the word Bob in Column B.

Some data is even more challenging to work with and requires multiple steps to convert.

For example, if you have "Smith, Bob, electrical engineer, Colorado" as your text string, you can't just specify space and comma as your delimiters. That will separate electrical engineer into two columns. You'd end up with "Smith", "Bob", "electrical", "engineer", and "Colorado" all in separate columns. If that same set of data also had an entry for "Jones, Mark, auditor, Nevada" you'd have a problem. Your state entry for Mark Jones would be lined up with the second part of the title entry for Bob Smith. Like below in Rows 17 and 18:

15					
16	**Example**	**Specify Comma and Space as Delimiter**			
17	Smith, Bob, electrical engineer, Colorado	Smith	Bob	electrical	engineer Colorado
18	Jones, Mark, auditor, Nevada	Jones	Mark	auditor	Nevada
19					
20		**Specify Comma As Only Delimiter**			**Apply TRIM Function to Remove Extra Space**
21		Smith	Bob	electrical engineer Colorado	Smith Bob electrical engineer Colorado
22		Jones	Mark	auditor Nevada	Jones Mark auditor Nevada
23					

All Excel knows is what you tell it. If you tell it that spaces and commas are delimiters, that's all it thinks about. It doesn't understand that that third entry is a title listing and that those words need to be kept together.

The better option, although it's also a two-step process, is to separate the data into columns using just the comma as your delimiter. That gives you entries that at least line up, but you'll still have an extra space in them like you see in Cells E21:H22 above.

But that's an easy fix. You can remove extra spaces around text using the TRIM function.

To trim the extra spaces from Cell E21 you can just type =TRIM(E21) in a cell. That's what I did above in Cell J21. I then copied the formula to cells J21:M22.

You can see that the extra spaces that were there in Cells F21:H22 are now gone.

To finish it off, copy cells J21:M22 and paste special-values so that the formulas are gone and all that's left is your listing of last name, first name, occupation, and location for each employee.

* * *

Always check your data after you convert it. Sometimes converting data is easy and all your entries convert without a hitch. But all it takes is one "Mark David Jones, III" in your list to throw things off.

THE CONCATENATE FUNCTION

Let's say what you really wanted to do was convert those "Bob Smith" entries to a "Smith, Bob" format. How would you do that? Or how would you take a column with first names in it and combine that with a column with last names in it to make an entry like "Smith, Bob"?

Enter the CONCATENATE function. The CONCATENATE function lets you combine multiple elements, including data across multiple columns, into one cell. How?

Let's just dive in and show you an example.

Below we have our first names and last names in separate columns and now we want to bring them together in the order "last name" + a comma + a space + "first name" where the last name is in Cell B2 and the first name is in Cell A2.

The formula for that is: =CONCATENATE(B2,", ",A2) which I've placed in Cell F2. I can now copy it down to Cells F3:F5 and we get:

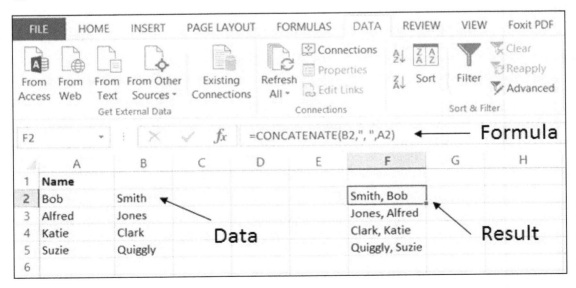

Right now all of the entries in Column F are still formulas. If we delete the contents of Columns A and B, we'll lose our values in Column F. So after I use CONCATENATE like this, I copy the cells where I used the formula and paste special – values to replace the formula with just the results of the formula so that doesn't happen.

Let's go back to that formula and break it down a bit, because it's important that you see what I did in that middle portion.

There are three elements that we're combining with that formula. First, the contents of Cell B2. Next, a comma and a space. And, finally, the contents of Cell A2.

To include the contents of a cell, you just list the cell name like I did with B2 and A2 in the formula.

To include text you need to use quotation marks around the text you want to include. In this example, I have a comma and a space within quotes for my second element.

So the formula is:

=CONCATENATE(

B2

,

" "

,

A2

)

If that's still a bit confusing to you, just try it a few times. Start with =CONCATENATE (B2, A2) which will give you SmithBob and then go from there to try and fix it.

Once you get the hang of it, CONCATENATE is very easy to use. The biggest challenge is remembering to include those text elements between cells when they're needed.

And you can put anything in between those quotes. If I need to include a / mark or a star or whatever else, I can.

Just remember: Excel will treat it as text.

If I write =CONCATENATE("=",A11,"*",B11) where A11=2 and B11=3, Excel will display that as =2*3. That's a text entry, not a formula, though. To turn it into a formula, you have to paste special-values and then click into the cell, copy the contents, and paste them into a new cell. So this is definitely not a shortcut for building formulas.

Bottom line: CONCATENATE lets you combine the values in different cells as well as text elements to create a single entry.

Now on to one of my favorite functions, the IF function.

THE IF FUNCTION

I love the IF function. I really do. That probably indicates a need for therapy, but it's true. I just…love it. It's so useful. Especially when you can nest IF functions. It's like building one of those complex flow charts, but in one cell.

So how do they work?

An IF function basically says, if A is true, then do B. If it isn't true, then do C.

When you nest IF functions, you can set something up that says if A is true then do B, if it isn't true then if C is true do D, and if that isn't true then if E is true do F, and if none of that is true do G. You can just keep going and going and going. It's awesome.

But you have to get it right.

So let's start with a basic IF function that looks at whether or not to charge shipping on an order. Let's say that all customers who buy more than $25 worth of product get free shipping and anyone who buys $25 or less worth of product has to pay a 5% charge for shipping.

Here's our data and our IF function:

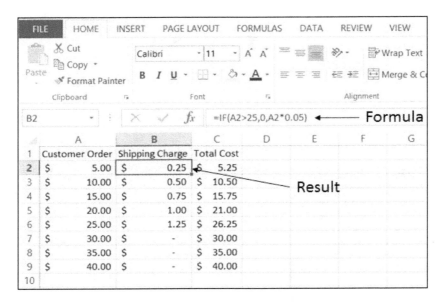

In Column A we have the cost of the customer's order. In Column B we have our IF function. For Row 2 it is =IF(A2>25,0,A2*0.05). In Column C we have the customer's total cost which is just Column A plus Column B.

Let's walk through the IF function.

The formula starts with IF A2 > 25. That's the condition we're evaluating. Did the customer spend more than $25?

The next portion of the function is 0. That's the outcome to return if the answer to the question we asked in the first part of the function is true. If our customer spent more than $25 then we want to return a result of zero.

The final portion of the function is A2*0.05. That's the outcome to return if the answer to the question is false. If your customer DID NOT spend more than $25 then we want to return a value equal to 5% of what they spent.

You can think of an IF function as walking through an if-then-else or if-then-otherwise process where each of the sections of the function is one of those steps. So: =IF(If, Then, Else)

IF A2>25, THEN 0, ELSE A2*.05.

That was just a simple IF function. Let's make it more complex. (This is where it gets fun.)

Let's say that we want to provide customers with a discount based upon how much they spend. Spend up to $25, no discount, over $25 and up to $50, $5, etc. To apply this discount, we can build a nested IF function. Here we go:

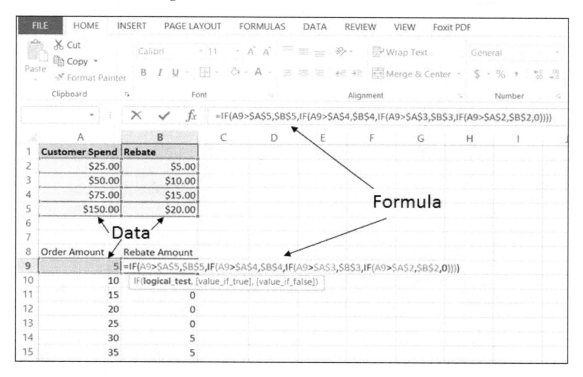

The table we want to use to determine our discount is in Cells A1:B5.

Our formula for an order amount that's listed in Cell A9 is:

=IF(A9>A5,B5,IF(A9>A4,B4,IF(A9>A3,B3,IF(A9>A2,B2,0))))

That looks insanely complicated, I know, but let's break it down. It's all just logical steps.

We start with IF A9>A5. Is the order amount over the value in Cell A5? (We use the $ signs here so we can copy the formula down to other cells and keep the references to the table constant.)

If that's true, then B5. That's our discount when the purchase amount is over the value listed in A5. So, if the customer paid more than $150 they'll get $20 off.

If that's not true, then…

We look to see if A9>A4. Instead of closing out the function with an alternate value, we start another IF function. This is the next step in our analysis. We know our purchase amount isn't greater than A5, but is it greater than A4?

If so, then B4. If it's not greater than A5 but is greater than A4, we apply the discount listed in B4. So all purchases for more than $75 and up to $150 receive a $15 discount.

If that's not true, then…

We look to see if A9>A3. Once more, instead of closing out the IF function, we start another one. Our value isn't greater than A5 or A4, but is it greater than A3?

If so, then B3. If it's not greater than A5 or A4 but is greater than A3, we apply the discount for purchases that are more than $50 and up to $75.

If that's not true, then…

Is A9>A2. This is our final threshold, so no more IF functions after this one. If our purchases is less than A5, A4, and A3 but still greater than A2…

Then, B2. We apply the discount for purchases over $25 and up to $50.

Otherwise 0. Because at that point the purchases is for $25 or less and there's no discount to apply.

Here it is again:

=IF(A9>A5,B5,IF(A9>A4,B4,IF(A9>A3,B3,IF(A9>A2,B2,0))))

* * *

It's kind of insane to walk through, right? It can seem overwhelming.

Draw it out if you need to. It's just IF-THEN-ELSE over and over again. The only difference is that the ELSE steps start over with a new IF-THEN-ELSE set of steps.

Sometimes, when I need to break an IF function like this down to figure out why it isn't working, I take out each of the individual IF functions and look at them separately. I start with the first IF function and ask what it's doing and why and if that makes sense. So what we had was:

=IF(A9>A5,B5,IF(A9>A4,B4,IF(A9>A3,B3,IF(A9>A2,B2,0))))

What if this wasn't working? How would you figure out where it's going wrong?

Start with the first IF function =IF(A9>A5,B5,OTHER) where OTHER is everything else that needs to happen after that.

Ask yourself, "Does it make sense that if A9 is greater than A5 we return a value of B5? And, if so, does it also make sense that if A9 is not greater than A5 that we do something else?"

When I originally was writing this IF function, I started with the lowest threshold instead of the highest. So I had =IF(A9>A2,IF(A9>A3,IF….and had ended with B2 as my last value. Take out all the garbage in between and I had IF(A9>A2,OTHER,B2). Meaning if A9 wasn't greater than A2 I was going to return a discount of $5. That was wrong. But to see it, I needed to get everything else out of the way.

For the curious, here's what it looks like to write an IF function that starts with the lowest threshold instead and works its way up.

=IF(A22>A2,IF(A22>A3,IF(A22>A4,IF(A22>A5,IF(A22>A5,B5),B4),B3),B2),0)

I prefer not to write IF functions like this one, because my mind doesn't follow the logic as well. In the example we walked through where you start with the highest discount, each IF function is completed before the next one starts. That's much easier to follow than this second approach where you're basically saying IF, IF, IF, IF, IF before you ever start in on your THEN, ELSE steps.

You can do it either way. And if you get stuck you can isolate each IF function to see what's wrong, but I just find the IF(A, B, IF(C, D,E)) approach an easier one to follow.

In addition to just getting the logic wrong, another error I commonly commit when building nested IF functions is failing to put enough parens or putting them in the wrong place. A few rules to remember:

1. Always have an opening paren after an IF.
2. Always have a closing paren after the last item for each IF function.

See this example again:

=IF(A22>A2,IF(A22>A3,IF(A22>A4,IF(A22>A5,IF(A22>A5,B5),B4),B3),B2),0)

See how after each of the price thresholds (B5, B4, B3, B2), we have a closing paren?
But it's different if you build it this way:

=IF(A9>A5,B5,IF(A9>A4,B4,IF(A9>A3,B3,IF(A9>A2,B2,0))))

In this case, each IF function is only closed out when the prior IF function is, so you end up with all of your closing parens at the very end.

We have four IF functions so need four closing parens.

Excel makes it easy to see if you have your parens in the right place. If you click into the formula bar and arrow through your equation Excel will highlight not only the paren you're on but it will also briefly bold the corresponding paren.

Also, Excel uses distinct colors for each set of parens, but those can be harder to see.

* * *

That was probably a lot to take in. So let's try to bottom line it:

- IF functions follow an IF-THEN-ELSE pattern.
- You can nest IF functions by replacing the THEN or the ELSE portion of an IF function with another IF function.
- If you get an error message that says you've entered too many arguments, the more likely cause is a misplaced paren.
- Always test your IF function after you've written it to make sure it's doing what you want it to do.
- If you're referencing a table of values that drive your IF function (like with our sales discount example), be sure to use $ signs to fix the cell references.

Alright, let's move on to COUNTIFS, another function I love. (Although not as much as I love SUMIFS which we'll cover after that.)

THE COUNTIFS FUNCTION

I probably use the SUMIFS function more than I use COUNTIFS, but I couldn't cover SUMIFS without also covering COUNTIFS.

For users of older versions of Excel, I know for a fact that the COUNTIFS and SUMIFS functions did not exist (before I believe Excel 2007) because I once used one of them on a work project and then had to go back and redo the entire worksheet when it turned out our client didn't have as recent a version of Excel as I did. So you may not have this function available if you're working in a pre-2007 version of Excel.

But I digress. (Again. Always.)

Let's get down to it.

What does COUNTIFS do?

If you use it on only one range of data, it will count the number of entries in that range that meet your criteria. If you use it on more than one range of data, for example, three columns, it will count the number of entries that meet all three of your criteria.

Let's look at a real-world example.

Here's our data and our calculations:

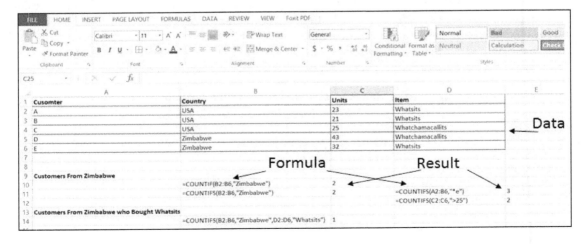

If you want to know how many customers you have in Zimbabwe, you can apply COUNTIFS to the column where you list the country for each customer, column B, using the equation:

=COUNTIFS(B2:B6,"Zimbabwe")

This basically says, look at the range from B2:B6 and count each time Zimbabwe appears.

(You could also use the COUNTIF function and get the same result, but might as well use COUNTIFS since it can be expanded to include more than one criteria.)

What if instead you want to know how many customers you have in Zimbabwe who also ordered Whatsits? Then you'd need to use COUNTIFS and set criteria for both Columns B, where you list country, and Column D, where you list product.

The equation is:

=COUNTIFS(B2:B6,"Zimbabwe",D2:D6,"Whatsits")

What you're saying here is, look at Cells B2:B6 and identify every time the value is Zimbabwe. For each row where the value in Column B is Zimbabwe, then look at the corresponding cell in Column D and see if that value is Whatsits. If it is, count it.

Both criteria must be met to be counted.

The COUNTIFS function isn't limited to exact word matches. You can use wildcards like the * in your count criteria. For example, =COUNTIFS(A2:B6,"*e*") will look for all cells where there's an entry with an e in it within the range and count it. In this case, that returned a value of 3, the two Zimbabwe entries as well as Customer E.

Note, too, that I had it count across rows and columns in that example. If you have multiple count criteria, though, they have to be the same size and orientation. You couldn't have A2:B6 and A3:A5, because those wouldn't match up in terms of size. And you couldn't have C2:C5 and A3:C3 together because they don't match up in terms of orientation. But you could have A1:B2 and C1:D2.

You can also use count criteria that are numeric. The function =COUNTIFS(C2:C6,">25") counts all entries in the range that have a value greater than 25. In this case, 2.

Another thing to keep in mind with COUNTIFS is that each range you specify needs to be unique. You can't use this to count entries where, for example, customers bought Whatchamacallits or Whatsits since in our example those are both listed in the same range.

If you select columns of data for your analysis then COUNTIFS will look across each individual row in that column to see if the criteria are met.

If you select rows of data for your analysis then COUNTIFS will look down each individual column to see if all criteria are met.

Here's another example of how it all works using three students and their scores on three exams.

F	G	H	I	J	K	L	M
	Student	Grade 1	Grade 2	Grade 3			
	A	92	82	88			
	B	93	94	93		←——— Data	
	C	93	92	93			
	Result		**Formula**				
	↓		↓				
Total Scores Over 90	7		=COUNTIFS(H2:J4,">90")				
# Test with All Over 90	1		=COUNTIFS(H2:J2,">90",H3:J3,">90",H4:J4,">90")				
# Student All Over 90	2		=COUNTIFS(H2:H4,">90",I2:I4,">90",J2:J4,">90")				

The formula in Cell G9, =COUNTIFS(H2:J4,">90"), is applying the COUNTIFS function across the entire range from H2 to J4 and counting any instance where the value is over 90. (I've copied the text of each of the formulas and pasted it into the cells in Column I using a ' to make it appear as text so you can see the formula and the result at the same time.)

The formula in Cell G9 returns a count of 7 because there were 7 test scores over 90.

The formula in Cell G10, =COUNTIFS(H2:J2,">90",H3:J3,">90",H4:J4,">90"), is applying the COUNTIFS function by rows to see how many tests there were where all three students scored over a 90. As you can see in the data, the only column where all three students scored over a 90 is for Grade 1 and that's the count it returns.

The formula in Cell G11, =COUNTIFS(H2:H4,">90",I2:I4,">90",J2:J4,">90"), is applying the COUNTIFS function by columns to see how many students had over a 90 on all three tests. As you can see in the data, this is true for students B and C which is why the count is 2.

COUNTIFS is very powerful, but as with a lot of these functions, it's easy to set it up wrong. One of the things I do when I'm building a worksheet using formulas like this is start small with data I can evaluate visually. I confirm that my function works the way I think it should before applying it to a larger data set where I can't easily confirm the result.

Once you have the basic framework down, you can then expand your formulas to cover a broader range of cells or to be more complex.

Start small. Test. Be sure you understand the concept and how it works. And then expand.

Alright, now on to SUMIFS which I use on a regular basis.

THE SUMIFS FUNCTION

Have I told you how much I love the SUMIFS function? Because I do. I use it all the time, primarily for tracking pending payments.

When I have sales of my books on Amazon it takes two months before I'm paid for those sales. In the meantime, I know that I'm owed X U.S. Dollars for sales in the U.S., Y Canadian Dollars for sales in Canada, Z British Pounds for sales in the UK, etc. I've had months where I had pending payments in at least six different currencies. Because of conversion rates, I can't just add those numbers together to see my total pending payments. 1 U.S. Dollar does not equal 1 Canadian Dollar and it certainly does not equal 1 Indian Rupee.

What I do to deal with this is use the SUMIFS function to sum all pending payments in each currency. I then apply a conversion rate to those amounts to see what I might actually be owed in U.S. Dollars. (Since currency exchange rates are constantly moving there's no actual guarantee that's what I'll receive in two months when I'm paid but at least it gives me a nice estimate. If you ever get big enough for those shifts to matter, look into currency hedging. I am not even close to worrying about that, though, so let's get back to the point.)

What does SUMIFS do?

It works much like COUNTIFS in that it looks to see if one or more criteria that you specify have been met. But where it differs is in what it does next. Instead of counting how many times all of those criteria are met it sums the values in a separate range of cells that you specify.

Let me show you how I use it. (Keeping in mind these are complete garbage numbers and not reflective of my actual earnings.)

| F2 | | | f_x | =SUMIFS(B$2:B$22,D$2:D$22,"USD",E$2:E$22,"") | | | |

	A	B	C	D	E	F	G	H
1	**Month**	**Income**	**Source**	**Currency**	**Paid**	**Total Outstanding**		
2	June 2017	$ 123.45	Amazon Brazil	BRL		$ 7,770.73	USD	$ 7,770.73
3	June 2017	$ 345.67	ACX	USD	X	$ 124.12	CAD	$ 93.46
4	June 2017	$ 546.78	Createspace	USD	X	$ 125.68	GBP	$ 177.71
5	June 2017	$ 124.68	D2D	USD	X	$ 1,246.35	EUR	$ 1,392.17
6	June 2017	$ 163.98	Nook	USD		$ 123.56	AUD	$ 92.79
7	June 2017	$ 698.43	Kobo	USD		$ 124.56	INR	$ 1.87
8	June 2017	$ 124.12	Authors Republic	USD	X	$ 123.45	BRL	$ 1.85
9	June 2017	$ 345.12	Google	USD	X			
10	June 2017	$ 125.23	Pronoun	USD				
11	July 2017	$ 124.47	ACX	USD	X	**Outstanding in USD**		$ 9,530.59
12	July 2017	$ 784.45	Createspace	USD				
13	July 2017	$ 31.25	D2D	USD				
14	July 2017	$ 315.27	Kobo	USD				
15	July 2017	$3,169.25	Nook	USD				
16	July 2017	$1,234.12	Pronoun	USD				
17	July 2017	$1,248.75	Amazon US	USD				
18	July 2017	$ 125.68	Amazon UK	GBP				
19	July 2017	$1,246.35	Amazon DE	EUR				
20	July 2017	$ 124.56	Amazon India	INR				
21	July 2017	$ 124.12	Amazon Canada	CAD				
22	July 2017	$ 123.56	Amazon AUS	AUD				

What you're seeing here is a listing of payments from sales channels. We have the sales month, the amount earned, the sales channel, the currency for the pending payment, and whether it's been paid yet. If you were to add all those values up they'd equal to 11249.29, but that number is useless. It means nothing because of the various currencies involved. Also, some of those amounts have already been paid so they're no longer outstanding.

Enter the SUMIFS function. In Cell F2 I have the formula:

=SUMIFS(B$2:B$22,D$2:D$22,"USD",E$2:E$22,"")

What that formula is saying is, for each row between 2 and 22 sum the values in Column B (amount earned) when the value in Column D (currency) is USD and the cell in Column E (Paid) is blank. Because I used $ signs to lock the cell references, I can copy that formula down and then just change the currency reference for each of the currencies in Column F.

The formula for Cell F6, for Australian Dollars, becomes:

=SUMIFS(B$2:B$22,D$2:D$22,"AUD",E$2:E$22,"")

Once I've broken out my pending payments by currency, I can then multiply them by the conversion rate for that currency to calculate an estimated amount that's outstanding in U.S. Dollars.

That's what's happening in Column H.

And then, last, but not least, I can add all those values together to get a total estimate of outstanding payments in USD.

That's not the only way I use SUMIFS. I also use it to track bills I've paid for the month and to calculate how much I still have due so I can make sure enough money is in my bank account.

You could also use this to sum, for example, the amount of payables you have outstanding from customers who are more than 30 days past due. Or the amount you've earned from customers who are in Zimbabwe. Or who are in Zimbabwe, whose account was opened by Salesman George, and where the account was opened within the last year.

Unlike with COUNTIF and COUNTIFS where you could use them interchangeably when dealing with one variable, the SUMIF and SUMIFS functions require you to enter your information in a different order, so you have to know which one you're using to write the function correctly. Since SUMIFS can handle anything SUMIF can, it's best to just stick with SUMIFS.

Also, like the COUNTIFS function, you can apply SUMIFS to ranges of cells, just be sure that the size and dimension of the ranges for each of the arguments (what to sum, what to evaluate) are the same or it won't work.

THE TEXT FUNCTION

I'll admit, I have not used the TEXT function a lot. It was never really on my radar until I recently had to figure out a way to convert a date to a day of the week so that I could recreate something I do in a more manual way as a pivot table. (For the time and word count tracking that's included in *Excel for Writers*.) But I have to say what I saw of it was very impressive.

According to Excel, the TEXT function "converts a value to text in a specific number format." That sounds pretty boring, doesn't it? You'd read that and think, "So what?"

But when you dig into it, it's far more interesting than that boring description would have you believe. It can do all sorts of things with formatting as well as providing detailed information about dates.

The basic way it works is you specify the cell to make into text and then provide the formatting you want. That cell you reference needs to be a number or a date for this to work, so it isn't a substitute for using CONCATENATE but they can do similar things.

At its most basic, TEXT can specify a format for a number.

You list the cell and then specify the format you want applied to the number in that cell. So =TEXT(E10,"$0.00") formats a number as currency with a dollar sign in front and with two decimal places.

There are a few tricks for formatting numbers:

Using a zero forces a specified number of decimal places to show even if the number doesn't require them. So, #.00 will display up to two decimal places even if that means displaying 2.00 or 2.50.

Using the pound sign (#) will display up to that number of decimal places, but will not force that many decimal places if the last number would be a zero. So, #.## would force 2.123 to be 2.12 but would leave 2.5 as 2.5.

Using a question mark (?) makes Excel insert spaces to align the decimal point across rows of numbers. You can substitute the question mark for a zero or combine it with zeroes to get the desired number of total decimal points to display. (But be careful. I used #.?0 and ended up with a number where the space was added to the question mark's location and it was then followed by a 0. Better to use #.0? instead to avoid that problem.)

Including a period in the text format will include a period with the number. Even when one isn't needed. So #.## applied to 2 gives you 2. which is not what you really want.

Here are some examples. The left- hand columns are sorted by number with white and gray bands to separate each one. The right-hand columns are sorted by format with white and gray bands to separate each format.

B2   *fx*   =TEXT(A2,"#.0#")

	A	B	C	D	E	F	G
1	Original Value	Converted Value	Format		Original Value	Converted Value	Format
2	1	1.0	#.0#		1	1	#
3	1	1.00	#.00		1.2	1	#
4	1	1.	#.?		1.7	2	#
5	1	1	#		2.356	2	#
6	1	1			1	1.	#.?
7	1	1.0	#.?0		1.2	1.2	#.?
8	1.2	1.2	#.0#		1.7	1.7	#.?
9	1.2	1.20	#.00		2.356	2.4	#.?
10	1.2	1.2	#.?		1	1. 0	#.?0
11	1.2	1	#		1.2	1.20	#.?0
12	1.2	1.2			1.7	1.70	#.?0
13	1.2	1.20	#.?0		2.356	2.36	#.?0
14	1.7	1.7	#.0#		1	1.0	#.0#
15	1.7	1.70	#.00		1.2	1.2	#.0#
16	1.7	1.7	#.?		1.7	1.7	#.0#
17	1.7	2	#		2.356	2.36	#.0#
18	1.7	1.7			1	1.00	#.00
19	1.7	1.70	#.?0		1.2	1.20	#.00
20	2.356	2.36	#.0#		1.7	1.70	#.00
21	2.356	2.36	#.00		2.356	2.36	#.00
22	2.356	2.4	#.?		1	1	
23	2.356	2	#		1.2	1.2	
24	2.356	2.356			1.7	1.7	
25	2.356	2.36	#.?0		2.356	2.356	
26							

See how using just the # sign to format a number results in that number being rounded up to the nearest whole number? (In Cells F2:F5)

Or how adding a ? after the period, but not including any zeroes in the format means you can end up with a whole number with a period after it? (In Cell F6)

Or how using "#.?0" adds a blank space between the period and the zero for a number like 1 to ensure that the decimal places line up? (In Cell F10)

And how using "#.00" forces a number to have two decimal places no matter what? (Cells F18:F21)

You can force pretty much any basic number formatting you want. But the additional benefit to using the TEXT function is that it also allows you to include text with that number formatting by using the & symbol.

For example,

$$=TEXT(E10,"\$0.00") \ \& \ " \text{ per unit}"$$

converts the numeric value in Cell E10 to a currency format with a dollar sign and two decimal places and then adds to that a space and the words "per unit". (If you want that space, it has to be within the quotes.)

That's very handy for when you have a series of numbers and you want to make them more presentation worthy.

But what has me really excited about the TEXT function is how it handles dates and times. Specifically, what it can do with months and days. You can take a date like 1/8/17 and using TEXT you can convert that into the name of the day of the week or the month. How cool is that?

Here's a list of examples:

K	L	M
Original Value	**Converted Value**	**Format**
1/8/2017	1	m
1/8/2017	01	mm
1/8/2017	Jan	mmm
1/8/2017	January	mmmm
1/8/2017	8	d
1/8/2017	08	dd
1/8/2017	Sun	ddd
1/8/2017	Sunday	dddd
1/8/2017	17	yy
1/8/2017	2017	yyyy
2:15:00 AM	2	h
2:15:00 AM	02	hh
2:09:00 AM	2:9	h:m
2:09:00 AM	2:09	h:mm
2:09:00 AM	2 AM	h AM/PM

In Cell L4 I've taken the date 1/8/17 and used the formula =TEXT(K4,"mmmm") to display the long version of the name of the month that corresponds to that date.

In Cell L8 I've used the formula =TEXT(K8,"dddd") to display the long version of the day of the week that corresponds to that date.

I don't know how often you'll need this, but it is pretty nifty and I did end up needing it for that pivot table. (Internet searches are your friend when you think something should be possible in Excel but have no idea how to make it work. Turns out there are no new problems under the sun, it's just a matter of knowing how someone else might phrase the question so you can find where it was already asked and answered.)

LIMITING ALLOWED INPUTS INTO A CELL

One of the biggest challenges with analyzing older data sets is that a lot of them didn't use standardized values. For example, one of the data sets I worked with started with paper forms that people completed by hand and that data was then input into a database exactly as it was written. Which meant that for a field like country you ended up with USA, U.S., Unites States, America, and all sorts of creative spellings of those words. When that happens, it becomes an incredible challenge to do any sort of analysis on that data set. You can't just say, count all entries where country is United States, because you'll miss all those other entries.

That's why if you're building any sort of tracking or input form you should limit the allowed values to the extent possible. Things like State and Country are obvious examples. But in the financial services industry you might also limit financial objective or income or net worth to pre-defined values or numeric ranges. Or, if you want exact numbers, at least limit the input field so that only numbers can be provided. If you don't, you'll end with someone somewhere who puts something like, "Refused to Disclose" in a net worth field.

So ask yourself, with the data you're dealing with, what can you standardize? Once you know that, if you're using Excel to track this kind of information, you can impose limits on those cells. You do this with Data Validation which can be found on the Data tab under Data Tools.

Let's walk through how to do it.

First, if you're going to have a list of acceptable values, you need to create it and have it available in Excel. I'd recommend putting it in another worksheet in the same Excel file. (We'll talk about how to hide that worksheet and lock it from editing later.)

Now that you have the list of accepted values (or if there is no list and you just want to limit the cells to a specific input type), highlight the cells you want to limit.

Next, click on Data Validation in the Data Tools section of the Data Tab and then Data Validation again.

You'll now see the Data Validation dialogue box.

If you're working with a list of accepted values, select List from the dropdown menu under Allow, and then click in the Source box and highlight your list of accepted values. You should end up with something like this:

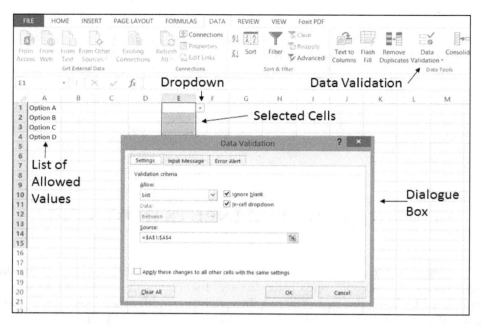

If you don't have a list of accepted values, you can choose under Allow to limit the formatting in those cells to Whole Numbers, Decimals, Dates, Times, a specific text length, or a custom format. When you choose one of those options it will require you to enter an allowed range of values. If you don't care what the range is, you can enter something like a minimum of 0 and a maximum of 1,000,000. (Although that example would force a positive number, so think through the implications of any range you choose.)

Click OK once you've made your choices.

For the list option, you'll see that the cells where you applied data validation now have a dropdown arrow. When you click on that arrow the only available choices will be the ones you specified. If someone tries to enter a different value in one of those cells, they'll receive an error message telling them the value they've entered is not valid.

The cells with number or text formatting limits won't have the dropdown arrow, but will generate an error message for any entry that doesn't meet your specifications.

You can add a message that will display when people click on any of the cells with data validation. Do so by using the Input Message tab in the Data Validation dialogue box.

You can also customize the error message by using the Error Alert tab.

To remove data validation, highlight the same set of cells, pull up the Data Validation dialogue box (by clicking on Data Validation and then Data Validation again under Data Tools in the Data tab), and choose Clear All in the bottom left corner.

One caution about using data validation. Be sure before you limit the inputs into a cell that you've thought through all the possible options. There is nothing more annoying than trying to input valid information and getting an error message and having no way to work around it.

I worked on a large project where we were trying to come up with these sorts of lists and when you really dig in, it isn't always as straight-forward as it seems. There are standardized lists out there for country, U.S. state, and currency code, for example, but sometimes the decision of which one to use is political. For example, do you list Burma or Myanmar? Where do you list Puerto Rico? How about including countries that no longer exist?

All I'm saying is think it through before you roll it out to your users, test it with them once you do, and then be open to making changes as needed. Unless there's a good reason not to, I like to include an Other option with a free-text field when I'm rolling out a new list. I then monitor to see what gets entered in that field so I can either update the list with an entry I missed, provide education to those misusing the Other field, or accept that there are sometimes one-off situations that will require that Other option to always exist.

LOCKING CELLS OR WORKSHEETS

Since we just talked about setting up a worksheet for someone else to use, it occurred to me you should also know how to lock a range of cells or hide a worksheet altogether. For example, I had a worksheet I created once for work where users input values into the first five or six columns and then those values were used in formulas that made up the rest of the worksheet. Because I didn't want anyone to change those formulas, I locked those cells down.

To lock a range of cells, first select the cells you want to lock, right-click, and choose Format Cells. In the Format Cells dialogue box, go to the Protection tab and click the Locked box. Then click on OK.

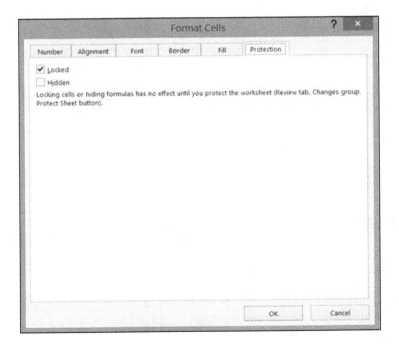

(If you also don't want users to even be able to see the formulas or values within those locked cells, you can also click on Hidden.)

The cells won't be locked at this point. You now need to add protection to the worksheet. To do that, go to the Cells section of the Home tab and click on Format. You should see an option to Protect Sheet. Select it and you'll see the Protect Sheet dialogue box.

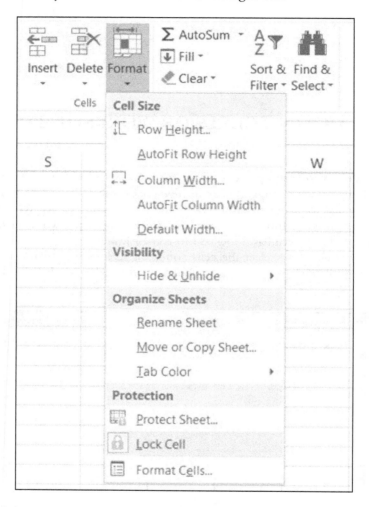

You need to use a password to lock the worksheet. Be sure you remember it.

There are a number of options for what you can allow users to do even when a worksheet is protected.

It's a little backwards since you're choosing what you're willing to allow instead of what you're not willing to allow, but there you have it.

The default is to allow people to select cells in the worksheet. Unless they shouldn't be copying the information for any reason, this is fine to keep.

I can also see an argument for allowing people to format columns in case they enter a value that's too big for the current column width, which I've had happen with users in the past. (It's very annoying to enter a number, see ### instead, and not be able to widen the column.)

What to allow from the rest of that list is a judgement call. I try to lock down as much as I can without interfering with functionality, so I'd probably lock too much and then wait for complaints and fix it then. It very much depends on the environment you work in. Is it better to allow users to do most everything and then find out that they do crazy things like delete the most important column in the worksheet? Or is it better to lock it down too tight and have to fix it when someone complains, which may damage your department's reputation and could, if you have the wrong kind of boss, lead to your boss yelling at you?

That's why beta testing is so important. Make your best choice and then give it to a bunch of users to test for you before you give it to everyone. See what they complain about and adjust from there. (That's the ideal scenario.)

Once you've protected a sheet, you'll see that the options that you didn't allow are no longer available in the menus and dropdowns.

To remove protection from a worksheet just go back to the Format dropdown, select Unprotect Sheet, and provide your password.

You can also add or remove protection on a worksheet or for an entire Excel file (workbook) on the Review tab in the Changes section using Protect Sheet or Protect Workbook.

HIDING A WORKSHEET

To hide an entire worksheet so that other users don't see it when they open the file (for example, if you have dropdown lists and you want to use one worksheet for storing them), right-click on the worksheet name and select Hide.

To unhide a hidden worksheet, right-click on the name of any worksheet that's visible, choose Unhide, and then select which of the hidden worksheets you want to unhide.

If you combine hiding a worksheet with protecting the workbook, no one will be able to access that hidden worksheet unless they have the password and can unprotect the workbook first.

CREATING A TWO-VARIABLE ANALYSIS GRID

This isn't a function within Excel, it's just something I find incredibly useful and often use Excel to do, so I figure it's worth sharing. It sounds far fancier than it is, too.

A two-variable analysis grid takes one variable (for example, hours worked) and another variable (for example, hourly wage) and creates a table showing the results of combining those two variables. I use it to look at potential income from consulting, to analyze income at different sales and price levels for my books, to calculate what I could earn if I sold my house at different prices and sales commissions, etc.

When you combine it with conditional formatting, it's even more powerful.

Let's look at an example using hourly wage and hours worked to see how just a little bit more income per hour can really add up.

	A	B	C	D	E	F	G	H
1		Weekly			Hours Worked			
2			10	20	30	40	50	60
3		$ 8.50	$ 85.00	$ 170.00	$ 255.00	$ 340.00	$ 425.00	$ 510.00
4		$ 9.00	$ 90.00	$ 180.00	$ 270.00	$ 360.00	$ 450.00	$ 540.00
5	Wages	$ 9.50	$ 95.00	$ 190.00	$ 285.00	$ 380.00	$ 475.00	$ 570.00
6		$ 10.00	$ 100.00	$ 200.00	$ 300.00	$ 400.00	$ 500.00	$ 600.00
7		$ 10.50	$ 105.00	$ 210.00	$ 315.00	$ 420.00	$ 525.00	$ 630.00
8								
9		Monthly			Hours Worked			
10			10	20	30	40	50	60
11		$ 8.50	$ 340.00	$ 680.00	$ 1,020.00	$ 1,360.00	$ 1,700.00	$ 2,040.00
12		$ 9.00	$ 360.00	$ 720.00	$ 1,080.00	$ 1,440.00	$ 1,800.00	$ 2,160.00
13	Wages	$ 9.50	$ 380.00	$ 760.00	$ 1,140.00	$ 1,520.00	$ 1,900.00	$ 2,280.00
14		$ 10.00	$ 400.00	$ 800.00	$ 1,200.00	$ 1,600.00	$ 2,000.00	$ 2,400.00
15		$ 10.50	$ 420.00	$ 840.00	$ 1,260.00	$ 1,680.00	$ 2,100.00	$ 2,520.00
16								
17		Yearly			Hours Worked			
18			10	20	30	40	50	60
19		$ 8.50	$4,420.00	$ 8,840.00	$13,260.00	$17,680.00	$22,100.00	$26,520.00
20		$ 9.00	$4,680.00	$ 9,360.00	$14,040.00	$18,720.00	$23,400.00	$28,080.00
21	Wages	$ 9.50	$4,940.00	$ 9,880.00	$14,820.00	$19,760.00	$24,700.00	$29,640.00
22		$ 10.00	$5,200.00	$10,400.00	$15,600.00	$20,800.00	$26,000.00	$31,200.00
23		$ 10.50	$5,460.00	$10,920.00	$16,380.00	$21,840.00	$27,300.00	$32,760.00
24								

Here I've created three grids, one that only looks at a week, one that looks at a month, and one that looks at an entire year. On the last one I've then applied conditional formatting to highlight any cells that are greater than $20,000. (I went with numbers close to the minimum wage, but obviously, you'd want to do this with numbers that were relevant to your own situation.)

This grid is incredibly easy to create. (I usually don't bother with all the fancy formatting.) All you need is to write your formula once in the first cell of the grid and then copy it to the other cells in the grid.

The formula I used in Cell C3 is =$B3*C$2

The formula I used in Cell C11 is =$B11*C$10*4

The formula I used in Cell C19 is =$B19*C$18*52

That's what you'd earn in a week, what you'd earn in four weeks, and what you'd earn in fifty-two weeks at that wage if you worked that number of hours.

Using the $ sign in front of the B makes sure that Column B continues to be the column referenced even when we copy the formula to the right. And using the $ sign in front of each of the row numbers (2, 10, and 18) makes sure that that's the row referenced even when we copy the formula down to other rows.

If I'd left those $ signs out and tried to copy the formula it wouldn't have worked when I copied it to other cells in the grid. All the other cells would have been referencing the wrong row or column. You could write each formula by hand, but why do that when you don't need to?

Here are the grids with formulas showing for the first two column options:

	A	B	C	D
1		Weekly		
2			10	20
3	Wages	8.5	=$B3*C$2	=$B3*D$2
4		9	=$B4*C$2	=$B4*D$2
5		9.5	=$B5*C$2	=$B5*D$2
6		10	=$B6*C$2	=$B6*D$2
7		10.5	=$B7*C$2	=$B7*D$2
8				
9		Monthly		
10			10	20
11	Wages	8.5	=$B11*C$10*4	=$B11*D$10*4
12		9	=$B12*C$10*4	=$B12*D$10*4
13		9.5	=$B13*C$10*4	=$B13*D$10*4
14		10	=$B14*C$10*4	=$B14*D$10*4
15		10.5	=$B15*C$10*4	=$B15*D$10*4
16				
17		Yearly		
18			10	20
19	Wages	8.5	=$B19*C$18*52	=$B19*D$18*52
20		9	=$B20*C$18*52	=$B20*D$18*52
21		9.5	=$B21*C$18*52	=$B21*D$18*52
22		10	=$B22*C$18*52	=$B22*D$18*52
23		10.5	=$B23*C$18*52	=$B23*D$18*52

That's it. It's that easy, but so powerful as an analysis tool. And, as you saw when we were talking about conditional formatting, you can incorporate additional fixed variables either in the formulas themselves (like I did here with the number of weeks) or by using a cell reference in the formula to point to the cells where you've entered them.

WHAT I HAVEN'T COVERED AND
HOW TO LEARN IT ON YOUR OWN

There are plenty of things you can do in Excel that I haven't covered here and didn't cover in *Excel for Beginners*. For example, there are hundreds of functions available in Excel and I've only covered maybe a dozen of them, all told. I could've provided a chapter on every single one, but most of what I would cover wouldn't be useful to most readers. I don't know anyone who has used all the function in Excel. I haven't and I've been using it as part of my day job for twenty-plus years.

What I've tried to do between this guide and *Excel for Beginners* is cover 99% of what the average reader will need in Excel. And, hopefully, give you a strong enough understanding of Excel that you can find the rest of what you need yourself.

Let me walk through how to do that.

Most of the options on the Excel toolbar have a description of what they do. All you have to do is hold your cursor over the option and it usually provides a one or two paragraph summary as well as a name for the option. Also, if there's a Ctrl shortcut, it lists that with the name. For example, Cut on the Home tab in the Clipboard section says "Cut (Ctrl+X)" and then has a description "Remove the selection and put it on the clipboard so you can paste it somewhere else."

If that isn't enough information, some of the options in Excel also have a "Tell me more" blue question mark at the bottom of that description. For example, Text to Columns in the Data Tools section of the Data Tab:

Text to Columns

Split a single column of text into multiple columns.

For example, you can separate a column of full names into separate first and last name columns.

You can choose how to split it up: fixed width or split at each comma, period, or other character.

 Tell me more

I consider this the best way to get into the Excel help screen for a given option. For some reason, when I try to search Excel help directly using the question mark in the top right corner of the screen it never seems to bring up what I want. But that is also another option. You can click on that question mark or press F1 and it will bring up the Excel Help box where you can enter a search phrase and then explore the suggested help topics to find what you want.

For functions, the best way to find more information is through the Insert Function dialogue box. To bring it up, go to the Formulas tab and select Insert Function.

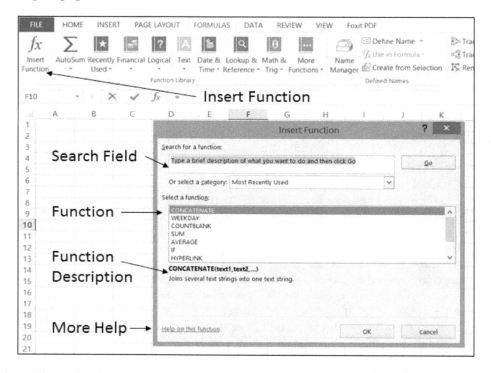

If you don't know the function you need, use the "search for a function" field. Type what you're trying to do into that box and click on Go and Excel will bring up a list of possible functions. For example, if I search for "merge text", CONCATENATE is on the list Excel provides.

Or you can use the dropdown menu below the search box to narrow your results to a specific type of function. (Financial, Math & Trig, Date and Time, Statistical, Lookup & Reference, Database, Text, Logical, Information, Engineering, Cube, Compatibility, Web, Most Recently Used)

If you do know the function, you can also type it in the search box.

For each function that Excel lists as a result of your search, when you highlight the function there will be a brief description of the function as well as, in the bottom left corner, a "help on this function" link.

If you need a better understanding of how the function works, choose the help link. This will bring up the Excel Help screen for that function.

Double-clicking on the function name will bring up a Function Arguments dialogue box that will walk you through how to build the function and will even show you a sample result.

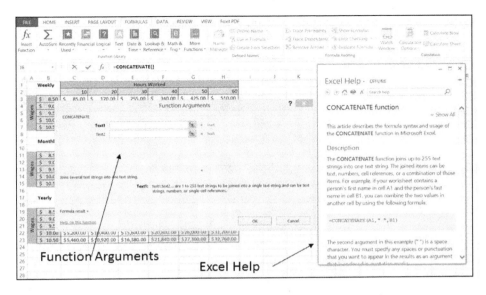

Function Arguments

Excel Help

Sometimes (often) none of the above will be enough to answer your question.

When I need to better understand a functionality within Excel, I usually use an internet search to get me to the correct page on the Microsoft website (support.office.com). I'll search for something like "pivot tables excel 2015" and then choose the search result for support.office.com. Don't ask me why, but the help Microsoft provides on its website is far superior to what it provides within Excel itself. There are sample data sets, step-by-step instructions, video tutorials, and all sorts of other learning aids. (A little late to tell you this now, but you could've probably worked your way through all of them and you'd know more than I've taught you. But no one ever does that. I certainly don't. I just go there when I'm stuck.)

What the Microsoft website isn't good at is telling you if something you want to do is possible or how to use a specific function for a specific purpose. So, for example, my two-variable analysis grid above. Microsoft, I don't believe, unless it's coincidental, isn't going to provide help on building something like that.

But someone somewhere has probably already asked if that's possible on an Excel forum. Something like, "I want to model the outcome of different combinations of two variables. How can I do that in Excel?" You can benefit from that by doing a quick internet search for something like "table combination two variables excel" and see what comes up. It isn't always perfect. Sometimes you have to adapt what someone else needed to your own purposes or wade through a bunch of arguments and incorrect answers to get what you need, but it's usually out there. (Don't click on any links provided in those answers, though. I don't trust that they aren't from scammers. If someone can't explain it right there in the forum, move on.)

You could also post your questions on one of those forums, but be prepared for some rough treatment if you do. Chances are you'll forget to mention the version of Excel you're working in or something else that the person answering your question considers essential, and instead of being polite about it they'll make some rude comment. And heaven forbid you post in the wrong forum…But if you tough all that out and give them what they need, you'll usually get a solution to your question.

Of course, you can also email me at mlhumphreywriter@gmail.com. I don't check that account daily, but I do check it regularly. If I know or can find the answer quickly, I will definitely help out. (Just don't ask me to build your entire tracking worksheet for you, not unless you're prepared to pay my consulting rate which is not cheap.)

CONCLUSION

That's it. That's *Intermediate Excel*. If you want to go beyond this to things like using macros or SQL, I'm afraid you're on your own. But I do hope that at this point you feel pretty confident that you can use Excel for day-to-day purposes and to do some more complex data analysis if nothing else.

I'm pretty sure I mentioned this in *Excel for Beginners*, but let me mention it again. If you're ever troubleshooting a formula or function, you can double-click on the cell that contains it and Excel will highlight all of the cells used by the function. It's often very easy to see that a function is referencing a blank cell, for example, instead of the one it needs to. You may not know how to fix that (although I'd like to think you will at this point), but at least you'll know enough to tell someone who can fix it what isn't working. Another thing to note about that is that Excel color codes the cell highlight and the cell reference within the function so you can see that a blank cell is being referenced and then look at the formula/function and see where that happens within the formula.

Anyway.

My other big piece of advice on all off this is two-fold.

First, remember that you can almost always undo things. Ctrl + Z is your friend. Don't be scared to try something. You can almost always undo it if it goes wrong.

Also, if you are building a worksheet with a lot of moving parts, be sure to save interim versions of it. So let's say I figure out how to get the calculation in Column A working perfectly and am now starting on a new calculation for Column B. I might save a version of my file and title it File20170830.xls and then keep working on Column B. That way if I mess things up so bad I can't fix them (it happens), I can just go back to that older file and start over from the point where I knew things were working. By using the YYYYMMDD date format in the file name, it also means I can easily sort my files by name and find the most recent version.

Take risks. Try new things. Remember, you can always undo it or go back to an earlier version if it doesn't work. Best of luck.

* * *

Also, if you want to test your knowledge of this material check out *The Intermediate Excel Quiz Book* which contains quizzes for each section of this book as well as five exercises that will allow you to apply what you've learned here in real-world scenarios.

ABOUT THE AUTHOR

M.L. Humphrey is a former stockbroker with a degree in Economics from Stanford and an MBA from Wharton who has spent close to twenty years as a regulator and consultant in the financial services industry.

You can reach M.L. at mlhumphreywriter@gmail.com or at mlhumphrey.com.

CPSIA information can be obtained
at www.ICGtesting.com
Printed in the USA
FFHW020410140519
52458380-57862FF